The Politics of International Monetary Reform— The Exchange Crisis

The Politics of International Monetary Reform—The Exchange Crisis

Michael J. Brenner

Written under the auspices of
the **CENTER FOR INTERNATIONAL AFFAIRS,** Harvard University

Ballinger Publishing Company • Cambridge, Massachusetts
A Subsidiary of J.B. Lippincott Company

This book is printed on recycled paper.

International Standard Book Number: 0–88410–292–0

Library of Congress Catalog Card Number: 75–45458

Printed in the United States of America

Library of Congress Cataloging in Publication Data

Brenner, Michael J
The politics of international monetary reform.

Bibliography: p.
Includes index.
1. Foreign exchange problem. 2. International finance. I. Title.
HG3851.B74 332.4'5 75–45458
ISBN 0–88410–292–0

Dedication

To Yvonne

Contents

Acknowledgments ix

Preface xi

Introduction 1

The Setting: National Politics and International Interdependence 3
Transgovernmental Cooperation 7
Central Banks and Treasuries 8
Politicization 13

Chapter One
The Crisis Unfolds 19

The Policy Problem 19
Background 20
The Analytical Problem: Adversity and the Decision Process 30

Chapter Two
Crisis Management 39

National Positions 42
Summary 65

Chapter Three
Negotiation 69

The March Emergency 70
The June-July Crisis 81

Chapter Four
The Theory and Practice of Flexible Exchange Rates 87

The Theory 88
Government Interpretation 99

Chapter Five
Implementing Flexible Exchange Rates 103

Managed Floating 104
Exchange Management and Domestic Policymaking 108
IMF Initiatives 112
Oil and Stagflation 114
Inflation 119
Floating—The Balance Sheet 122

Conclusion 129

Central Bank Collaboration 132
Theorists and Practitioners 138
Morale and Prospect 140

Index 143

About the Author

Acknowledgements

In the preparation of this book, I have incurred, happily, a debt of gratitude to many people whose cooperation and assistance warrant more than the conventional expression of appreciation that I can offer here. Raymond Vernon and Samuel Huntington, director and associate director of the Center For International Affairs at Harvard University, staked me to the venture capital for inaugurating this study and made available the facilities of the center. Professor Vernon also commented at length on an earlier version of the manuscript. A special word of thanks goes to Professor Benjamin Friedman of Harvard and to James L. Burtle of W.R. Grace & Co., who did much to help unscramble the thoughts of a neophyte in the world of international economics.

Officials, in the United States and abroad, were generous in their time and unfailingly solicitous of my scholarly enterprise. I trust that my account does justice to their intelligence and ability. They include Andrew Brimmer, former governor of the Federal Reserve Bank; Ralph Bryant, Director of the International Division of the Federal Reserve; Samuel Y. Cross, U.S. Executive Director at the International Monetary Fund; Robert Soloman, Adviser to the Federal Reserve's Board of Governors and former Secretary of the Committee of Twenty; Paul Volcker, former Under Secretary of the Treasury and now President of the Federal Reserve Bank of New York; and Charles Coombs, retired manager of the Federal Reserve's foreign desk, who provided me with invaluable insight into the nature of central bank cooperation and operations. In Europe, I wish to mention Milton Gilbert, Economic Adviser to The Bank for International Settlements; André de Lattre, Sous-Directeur of the Banque de France; Félix Le Norcy, formerly of the Banque de France; Antoine Seillère, member of the *cabinet* of Foreign Minister Michel Jobert; Professor Raymond Aron, Collège de France; Christopher MacMahon, Executive Director of the Bank of England; and Charles A.E.Goodhart of the Bank's Economic Intelligence Division; and Dr. Rieke of the Deutsche Bundesbank. At the IMF, Joseph Gold, general counsel; Jacques J. Polak, economic counsellor; and Hans O. Schmidt, the UK deputy,

I benefitted greatly as well from numerous useful discussions with the following economists and directors at commercial banks: Harold vanB. Cleveland, Citibank; John Cooper, Singer & Friedlander (London); John Forsyth, Morgan Grenfell (London); Herr Hanselmann, Union de Banques Suisses (Zurich); Robert LeClerc, Continental Illinois; Dr. Hans J. Mast, Crédit Suisse (Zurich); Robert Piloy, Société Générale de Banque (Brussels); J. Shepard Poor, Morgan & Co. International (Paris); and Alan Teck, Chemical Bank. Journalists too were not spared my attentions. Marjorie Deanne, *The Economist*; Robert Kleiman, *The New York Times*; Charles Stabler, *The Wall Street Journal*, and Philip Whitcomb, *The Christian Science Monitor* offered me both their hospitality and their very considerable knowledge. Among the academic economists who were admirably tolerant of a trespasser of discipline boundaries were C. Fred Bergsten, The Brookings Institution; Benjamin J. Cohen, The Fletcher School; Hendrik Houttaker, Harvard; Charles Kindleberger, MIT; and Fritz Machlup, Princeton University. I particularly wish to thank Professor Machlup for his kindness.

In keeping with the tradition or heroic authorship, I hereby absolve all of the above gentlemen, and lady, of any responsibility for the end to which I put their ideas and advice.

Michael J. Brenner
New York City
November 1975

Preface

International monetary affairs is not a subject that has excited the interest of political scientists. Even students of world politics have viewed it as a vaguely alien and impenetrable intellectual territory. There is something mystifying about the arcana of exchange rates, adjustment mechanisms, forward and spot money markets. Understandably, they have been looked upon as the proper preserve of the *cognoscenti* conversant with the monetary domain's recondite ways and daunting economic theories.

There also has been little practical incentive to venture into these uncongenial precincts. The network of institutions implanted after World War II to facilitate commercial and financial interchange was seemingly well tended by the most astute and reliable of public servants. The great prosperity of the Western world was the unmistakable fruit of the system's success. Occasionally there would be a brief flutter of crisis as some improvident currency suffered through the throes of devaluation. None seemed serious enough to disturb the confident belief that matters were well in hand. Much has changed. In recent years, the international economy has suffered severe dislocations. Disquietude about the stability and future effectiveness of the monetary system in particular is pervasive. It is nourished by doubts as to whether the old formulas are still valid. A good deal of the magic is gone from the wands of economic policymakers and with it the abundant faith in the practical achievements of collective institutions.

For the analyst of international relations, there is the recognition of an obviously important subject in need of attention. The issues revealed are very much political: how to formulate and affirm a common international purpose; the constraints and conflicts of national sovereignty; the relationship of technical assessment to political decision. Inhibitions about trespassing academic boundaries are less keenly felt when the inadequacies of economic analysis are apparent, and the judgment of policymakers arbitrates specialists' debates.

It is not surprising therefore that political economy is making a comeback. This study is intended as a modest contribution to that revival. It deals with the breakdown of the regime of fixed exchange rates established at Bretton Woods, and the subsequent effort at redesigning an adjustment mechanism for the international monetary system. The introductory chapter states the main themes and lays out the approach that will be used for analyzing the process of collective economic decisionmaking. It notes the contradictory pressures placed on national leaders by the compulsions of domestic politics and the requirements for international stability. The task of reconciling them is complicated by the present uncertainty in conceptualizing an ambiguous and changing reality. To highlight these issues a comparison is drawn between Treasury Secretaries and central bank directors. The latter are of particular interest since they enjoy a modicum of political autonomy and collaborate to perform specific functions on behalf of the international monetary order.

Chapter One has two purposes. First, it recounts the collapse of the exchange markets in March 1973 and sketches the background to the crisis. Then a number of hypotheses are presented about the way governments address a problem of crisis management. They point up the multiple influences that combine to fashion an official's perception of the problem and conjecture which officials, under what circumstances, are most inclined to take an internationalist approach.

Chapter Two reviews in detail the thinking and strategies of the major financial and trading nations involved in the crisis. It examines the interplay of economic interest, ideology and political aims in defining national positions. The negotiations leading to the introduction of flexible exchange rates are examined in Chapter Three. The conflicting interpretations of what the new system promised and the disagreements over the desired form that coordinated management should take are considered in Chapter Four. A summary of the intense debate over floating rates is offered, and the alliance of theory and interest discussed. Chapter Five analyzes the workings of existing arrangements. It is especially concerned with the extent and shape of the intergovernmental cooperation it demands and its implications for the role of monetary authorities. The chapter also presents a balance sheet evaluating the performance of flexible exchange rates. The

Conclusion reconsiders the study's main themes in the light of the exchange crisis. It emphasizes the obstacles to major renovation of an unstable monetary system inherent in a condition of selective interdependence and the difficulties of making economic theory proximate to political choice.

Introduction

In March 1973 the governments of the leading financial and trading nations agreed to amend fundamentally the international monetary system by establishing the principle of flexible exchange rates. The abandonment of fixed par values among national currencies represented a major departure from the Bretton Woods accords which since World War II have set the rules for world monetary management. The emergence of floating rates as the preferred solution to the outstanding problem of international financial life, and its acceptance as the system's adjustment mechanism, offers a rare opportunity to consider the circumstances and requirements for policy innovation and collective decisionmaking in a primary area of interstate economic cooperation.

Coming in the wake of a dramatic breakdown on the money markets, the agreement was the culmination of a protracted period of crisis, a period during which Treasury and central bank authorities had struggled, with mounting urgency and diminishing success, to reestablish control over currency exchanges beset by disruptive speculative forces. They sought to restore exchange stability as an essential component of the global economic infrastructure on which their common prosperity depended and for whose well-being they were collectively responsible.

This study examines that process of intellectual adjustment and policy initiation. It has two main themes. One concerns the interplay of domestic and international pressures that act on government officials who are charged simultaneously with safeguarding the national welfare and maintaining a durable framework for world economic activity. With the exchange rate issue serving as empirical anchor, I shall consider how different sets of actors undertake to bring into focus the two partially overlapping spheres of policymaking, reconciling particular national interests with recognized system needs. The key questions are: To what extent is the objective reality of growing interdependence reflected in shared images among the government leaders who work the system? What are the practical considerations of interest, or notions of rank and status, that determine their readiness to accent the collective dimension of their relationship *or*, rather, to pursue policies aimed at fulfilling purely national ambitions? Within governments, are there appreciable differences in how officials in the various economic departments—each with its special organizational missions—frame the issues at hand, define their country's interests, and fashion policy proposals?

To help answer these questions, I shall contrast the outlook and approach of central bank authorities, who share specific tasks in administering collective monetary arrangements, and that of their colleagues in Treasuries or Finance Ministries. The comparison should give more concrete meaning to theoretical issues about a postulated diminution of national governments' exclusive decision-making powers, their consonant sensitivity to external forces, and the opportunities presented for subgovernmental units and bureaucratic actors to initiate or deflect policy innovations. Is there an internationalist orthodoxy common to central bankers? Are their judgments of national economic benefit influenced by the obligation to make them in reference to general needs and the counterpart interests of collegial states? On the exchange issue, did their views differ markedly, and consistently, from officials elsewhere in government? Is there evidence of attempts at concerting their positions in order to persuade governments to take a particular course of action?

The second theme is the intellectual response to the challenges of political-economic problem solving. The normal difficulties of negotiating collective agreements are complicated when existing formats have proven faulty and prevailing ideas have to be modified or adapted to changing circumstances. Often, disagreements as to the nature of the economic reality being confronted (and the correct theory for conceptualizing it) poses more formidable obstacles to accord than do conflicts of interest. It is hard enough to resolve disputes and agree on a program for reform when the participants can readily identify criteria for choosing among alternatives—i.e., when they know with some assurance what steps will produce what results. When these cause-and-effect connections are obscure, and the outcomes unpredictable, the opportunity costs of trying to upgrade the common interest through radical innovation are even more likely to overshadow the hoped for gains to each participant.

This study will specify how conflicting perceptions of the means-end relationship in international monetary affairs stand in the way of efforts to reconcile the substantive interests of national governments. It will show how high uncertainty in dealing with what often are indecipherable economic conditions affects the preferences of governments, and the trade-offs of divergent goals in advocacy and decision. In doing so, we shall be raising questions as to the relative importance of a nation's history, social philosophies, and economic circumstance in shaping its perspective on international economic issues; the differences of outlook that are discernible among departments of government; the affinities between technical analyses and an individual's, or country's, value preferences; and how the terms of the international policy debate are set by these diverse perspectives.

Another facet of the intellectual response to economic adversity concerns the activities, and influence, of nongovernmental experts. Floating exchange rates was a departure in both theory and practice. There is an undeniable connection between abstract academic theory and the usually more simplified conceptions of policymakers, but it is an elusive one to pin down. Theorists and practitioners differ in viewpoint and responsibility. The insistent logic-chopping and formal exegesis of the former are at variance with the latter's inherent pragmatism. Moreover, subjective judgments permeate the expert's prescription of a remedy (and an official's evaluation of the advice he receives). In proposing, or reviewing, policy alternatives, a host of personal judgments must be made with regard to all of the following: the cause-and-effect relationship between a specified action and an intended result, the final sum of contradictory or offsetting consequences, the capabilities and trustworthiness of governments, and not least, the relative value of different social goals.

THE SETTING: NATIONAL POLITICS AND INTERNATIONAL INTERDEPENDENCE

The debates of recent years over the structure, operation and performance of the world's monetary system have taken place in the generally optimistic context of postwar prosperity. They have focused on problems, such as the proper exchange rate mechanism, that have been at once witness to and the product of the very considerable success achieved under the Bretton Woods system. Unprecedented economic progress among the Western industrial countries owes much to the confidence afforded by the institutions created after WW II—e.g., the International Monetary Fund (IMF), the General Agreement on Trade and Tariffs (GATT), the Organization for Economic Cooperation and Development (OECD). These institutions today are victims of their own success, now to be modified or superseded. Determining the form, and the extent, of the necessary changes, though, poses a dilemma.

It has been the same rapid increases in the movements of trade and capital they facilitated that, in the 1960s, began to make apparent the need for alteration and/or elaboration of existing procedures and institutions. The creation of Special Drawing Rights (SDRs) as an embryonic international money, the long menu of proposals for stabilizing the growth of international liquidity, the refining of arrangements for concerted central bank borrowings and currency interventions, and efforts to lower tariffs and dismantle nontariff barriers to trade—as well as the design of a new exchange rate system—have been predicated on continuation of a regular, roughly parallel advance in economic growth among the industrial nations of the West, progress these reforms meant to encourage.

There were two concomitant political ingredients in this positive view of what, from any historical vantage point, has been a uniquely effective and smooth system of economic exchange. One was confidence in the orderliness and stability of internal political life and in the enlightened governmental leadership identified with postwar prosperity. The other has been the dominant position of the United States, which could direct—for better or worse—and often make decisions on behalf of the like-minded Western nations that constituted an elite club overseeing the system's operation and managing its collective institutions. By degrees, both of these conditions are changing—introducing a new fluidity, and indecisiveness, into deliberations over the reform of that network of rules, formats and conventions grown up over the past thirty years.

America's role, while still preeminent, has been steadily reduced. The 1971 devaluation of the dollar, along with suspension of its convertibility into gold, were symbolic acts publicly proclaiming that the era of U.S. monetary stewardship was over. It provided the most vivid evidence of a wider trend that has seen the emergence of strong commercial competitors, and a partial shift in the locus of financial power toward her European partners. (More recently, complacency has been rudely disturbed by challenges from producers of basic commodities and aggressive claims by the poorer developing countries). This progressive dispersion of economic strength has accompanied, and in some respects encouraged, the scaling down of Washington's global aspirations. As the hegemonic state, the U.S.

enjoyed both the constructive power of forcing solutions she saw as in the best interests of the Western world as a whole, and the negative power of preventing changes she deemed antithetical to her own—and therefore the system's—well-being. The United States no longer has the power to assert these hegemonial prerogatives—although there remains the tendency to assume the synonimity. Recognition of her finite capacities has dulled the American appetite for ventures in international construction. Conversely, the unresponsiveness of a decentralized system (and the intractability of its problems) to American initiatives has provided a sense of absolution from selfless responsibility and a license for indulgence of mercantalist inclinations [1].

The international monetary system no longer depends on a benevolent American guardianship. Nor does it derive the benefits of the earlier hegemony. The primary deficiency revealed in these recent years of irresolute monetary reform is the absence of a leader able, or willing, to force renovation of cooperative institutions increasingly in need of repair. Consequently, innovation is hostage to the vagaries of multilateral negotiations, with all their attendant pitfalls.

In this situation, the foremost obstacle to reform is that serious attempts at renewal, to meet the new conditions of sensitive interdependence, are seen as threatening to undercut national powers of economic management. Government officials and students of international affairs alike have become progressively aware of the contradictions and strains inherent in a condition of deepening interdependence where the superintending authority is divided among sovereign states each with its special interests, vulnerabilities and social philosophies [2]. The problems of maintaining that complex system of economic interchange are comprehensive in scope (if not uniform in effect and saliency), but the power to deal with them is fragmented and parochial. There is now a pronounced discrepancy between, on the one hand, the requirements for stability and optimal performance for the system viewed as an aggregate whole, and, on the other, the constraints imposed on governments by the exigencies of local circumstance.

For more than a generation maximizing production and arranging distribution have been taken as self-evidently what modern society and its public institutions are all about. The former task in this tandem undertaking—economic steering—is becoming technically more challenging thanks in good part to the impingement on domestic policy of imperfectly controlled, and incompletely understood, international forces. The problem is sharpened by the mounting evidence that governments are feeling more, rather than less pressure by economic associations to promote their interests. The readiness to initiate measures to master these global elements—e.g., large sums of speculative capital in private hands, the activities of multinational corporations—in the manner that internal economic forces have been is inhibited by governments' ever present obligations to assure uninterrupted increases in reward for all those sectors of society on whose support their political viability depends. The very success in routinizing prosperity seemingly has not created the authority which could be used to assure that achievement is more solidly grounded on a new set of stable international agreements. As income levels and standards of living rise, appetites become keener and apprehensions grow about any break in the linear growth in wealth—however temporary, and however limited the numbers affected. Material success has produced not confidence, but anxiety, insecurity and a more compulsive acquisitiveness [3].

As a result, public officials perceive themselves as living on the thin edge of rejection, vulnerable to the withdrawal of backing by any significant coalition of groups and factions that feel themselves disadvantaged by a turn of economic events. Hypersensitive as they are to any slowdown in the rate of growth, postponement of increases in disposable private income, or grievances of a sector adversely affected by a shift in policy or markets, there is an attendant narrowing of a leader's margin for exercising discretionary powers of judgment, decision and initiative. The consequence can be acceptance of severe temporal and latitudinal constraints.

Of course, leaders are not entirely slaves to interest politics. Every system secures for its leadership a range of discretionary authority applicable to high affairs of state, defense and foreign policy more conventionally defined. It is in the grey areas, such as international economics, where the stakes might well dictate applying these discretionary powers and yet where the nature of the issues fails to evoke the attitude of deferential support necessary for launching difficult initiatives, that the liabilities of this modus operandi are most apparent. Indeed, there often is the disposition to transpose onto the international plane elements of the domestic interest and status competition in ways that run directly counter to the logic of global economic order.

This situation is not lacking in irony. As governments are uncomfortably aware, their ability to control events and to produce results is weakening due to the growing importance of international forces that lie on the margins of their control. Yet their mastery would require the extension of international regulatory institutions, encroaching upon the domain of fiscal and monetary management, that governments still consider an exclusive national preserve. Budgets, tax schedules and rediscount rates have been the effective weapons used by governments to routinize prosperity for the past quarter century. Their proposed relegation to extranational bodies can but accentuate feelings of vulnerability. Of lessened utility in dealing with structural problems that are reflected in and influenced by the external environment, they still seem the best and only means at hand. For governments are not prepared to relinquish their fate either to an international authority or to the depoliticized workings of the world's markets, even if unable to avoid constant reference to the global setting of domestic policymaking.

TRANSGOVERNMENTAL COOPERATION

Routine consultation and collaboration among officials, for whom interdependence is an inescapable fact of contemporary government, is a feature of this equivocal situation. The scope and detail of their mutual responsibilities, their critical importance for achieving national ends, and, frequently, the development of close personal ties points to an exceptional type of intergovernmental exchange. They raise the question as whether these networks have a serious bearing on the deliberation of common problems, pushing outcomes further in the direction of collective solutions than the conventional processes of interstate negotiation ordinarily would [4]. To put it somewhat differently, do these networks serve as the instrument through which a practical expression is given to common system needs—e.g., avoiding excessive, inflationary, liquidity growth—that is greater than the sum of its nationally self-interested parts—gaining ready access to credit for financing deficits?

In formulating this issue, Keohane and Nye have dubbed these cross-national ties *transgovernmental*—i.e., "sets of direct interactions among sub-units of different governments." In some instances, where they are "not controlled or closely guided by the policies of the cabinets or chief executive of those governments," it is suggested, officials might be in a position to take advantage of the waffles and ambiguities of central policies to influence significantly the course of action [5]. In less pliable circumstances, collegiality can still nurture shared attitudes that "permit the development of more flexible bargaining behavior." Basically, Keohane and Nye postulate two kinds of transgovernmental behavior. "Transgovernmental *policy coordination* refers to activity designed to facilitate smooth implementation or adjustment of policy, in the absence of detailed higher policy directives. Another process, *transgovernmental coalition building*, takes place when sub-units build coalitions with like-minded agencies from other governments against elements of their own administrative structures" [6]. Potentially, then, the impact of routinized collaboration among national officials is seen as ranging from active collusion "to determine a government decision" or a concerted strategy to deviate from the declared position of central foreign policy organs, through milder joint efforts at inflecting the outcome by "structuring the policy agenda," to the more modest consequence of sensitizing officials to the internal conditions faced by their foreign colleagues and shaping policies to facilitate implementation [7].

The writings on transgovernmentalism draw intellectual sustenance from recent theorizing about bureaucratic politics [8]. It has become a commonplace of political analysis that governments are not unitary actors, that power is fragmented and policy responsibility distributed among executive departments and agencies—each with its own missions, organizational interests and constituencies. A policy decision is viewed as the outcome of bargaining among these bureaucratic actors. In some instances, governmental agencies act to favor the interests of those economic sectors whose welfare is their administrative charge. In others, the impulse toward bureaucratic games playing derives from the organization's preoccupation with expanding its critical functions, protecting a jurisdictional claim, or advancing careers and establishing status by putting its mark on national policy.

The strength of bureaucratic considerations in the policy process is variable. The correctness of the paradigm is a matter of degree. Some of the theory's apostles, carried away by their discovery that policymaking is not tidy and systematically rational, have staked the intellectual claim that governmental action will be dominated, unavoidably and immutably, by bureaucratically defined interests and perceptions of national welfare. This drastic conclusion, though, has not been substantiated, either in the area of national security policy (where its roots lie) or in other, nonmilitary spheres. Any application should prudently refrain from a priori assumptions of analytic truth. In transposing the bureaucratic politics model onto the domain of international monetary relations, we should be especially sensitive to the dangers of reification since, by virtue of their technical complexity, the issues can too readily give the impression of being the natural preserve of technocratic functionaries.

CENTRAL BANKS AND TREASURIES

These ideas about transgovernmental politics at first glance seem to have most immediate reference to central banks. For there are features of central banking that lend a special flavor to their policy role—their relative autonomy from elected office holders (a status that varies in degree from country to country); their operational responsibilities for collaborative monetary management; and the sense of mutual obligation they share. They are pivotal figures acting at the interface of domestic and international policymaking, performing functions at the margins of the political and bureaucratic.

As supervisor of domestic monetary affairs, a central bank director is charged with critical functions—determining the proper annual increase in the money supply, fixing interest and rediscount rates, setting reserve margins, and monitoring private bank operations. He is a main actor in the constant, intricate and challenging game of economic steering. Its challenge derives from the complexity of contemporary economic life, the imperfection of our theories for comprehending and controlling it, and also the participation of the several governmental agencies and numerous other organized interests with a substantial stake in the outcomes. Moreover, external economic forces have come to bear in more direct and powerful ways on the job of directing the national economy, through capital flows—motivated by interest rate differentials, investment opportunities or tax structures—that affect the stock of money, income and price levels; through trade patterns affecting exports, imports and the internal distribution of resources; through exchange rate pressures and payments balances; and through foreign government policies directed at all of these. It follows that world conditions, and questions of their collective oversight, figure prominently in the deliberations that unfold in cabinet rooms and council chambers.

Central banks have a unique, if usually inconspicuous, role in the ensuing effort to bring the external environment into harmony with domestic conditions, for they have been called upon to assume specific undertakings on behalf of world monetary stability, as stipulated for them under the Bretton Woods system and modified by the practice of a generation—to intervene with reserves on the exchange markets to maintain currency rates within a specified band; to arrange multilateral credit lines to finance short or longer term deficits, either through the IMF or the Bank for International Settlements (BIS) in Basle, in the form of "swap" facilities; to act jointly with other monetary authorities to coordinate capital controls and interest rates. In order to perform these functions, they are in routine contact with their counterparts in other capitals and meet periodically in the several consultative forums created for the purpose [9]. The satisfactory performance of his functions in either of these complementary policy spheres depends appreciably on what occurs in the other and on the ability of officials to exercise a degree of control over developments in each. A further inference is that for a central bank director to retain an active and respected voice in the councils of his government, he must demonstrate that he is cognizant of, and reasonably successful in fulfilling, national needs in the international environment. This means both meeting overall system objectives—adequate liquidity created to permit growth of commerce, stability assured on the exchange markets to protect against disruptive rate changes—*and* doing so in ways that protect the special interests and position of his country. Conversely, to perform his system maintenance duties internationally, he must be assured of (1) the willingness of his political superiors to support the measures requisite for collective management to work, and (2) the power to set domestic monetary policy (interest rates, money creation) so that it coincides with, or at least does not contradict, joint intergovernmental programs (exchange interventions in support of a weak currency). To the extent that these orientations are mutually reinforcing (as in controlling speculative capital waves), the task is that much easier. On those occasions when they diverge, and the two impulses pull in opposite directions, the predicament of collective decisionmaking is heightened.

To phrase it another way, monetary authorities must reconcile the zero-sum and the nonzero-sum dimensions of international relations. Implicit in the distinction we are drawing between central bankers and Economics Ministers is the hypothesis that the former are oriented more toward the nonzero-sum aspects of the system. Their explicit international responsibilities do at least imply a greater concern for the framework of cooperative monetary relations. It remains to be determined, though, whether the practical result is a distinctive approach to issues or simply a variation of attitudes general to their governments.

The strain between the national and the collective interest is also felt, if in somewhat diluted form, by a Treasury Secretary, Treasury officials are less directly engaged in collaborative activities. But they too must design strategies that maximize their chances for meeting their paramount objective—generating prosperity—while simultaneously acknowledging internationally defined commitments (and yet doing so in a manner that safeguards essential powers of national decisionmaking). A Treasury Secretary (or Minister of Economics, or Chancellor of the Exchequer),* along with his senior staff, normally

*For convenience we shall use the terms "Treasury Secretary" and "Economics Minister" interchangeably in referring to the cabinet officer who directs economic policy.

has primary responsibility for fashioning economic policy. It is his hand that holds the tiller; it is he who sets the course after receiving advice, solicited or otherwise, from his fellow officers; and it is he who gets periodic instructions from the political captain in the President's or Prime Minister's chair who establishes the goals and monitors progress toward them. Orchestrating the now universally accepted fiscal and monetary tools of aggregate demand management—budgetary expenditures, tax rates, credit terms—he attempts to steer the economy on an even keel between the twin dangers of recession and excessive inflation. Like a prudent helmsman, he leans the ship into the wind, expanding or contracting, encouraging now public expenditure, now private spending, now savings and investment, as the economy's movement dictates. He is expected to succeed.

His timing, and his selection of instruments in pursuit of the elusive goal of stable growth with price stability cannot avoid being influenced by the external commercial and financial environment. In the normal course of things, governments must review and evaluate how the whole complex of interdependent ties is affecting national economic performance and domestic welfare. Monetary conditions become prominent in a variety of ways. Capital inflows might be inflating the monetary supply or outflows squeezing investment funds, contrary to the direction of domestic policy; a trading partner's devaluation is threatening the export sector, or his upward revaluation aggravating inflation by raising import prices. For the period of monetary crisis we shall be examining, the crux of the policy problem was payments imbalances. If a country was running payments deficits, it had to decide which remedial steps, in what combinations, were technically feasible, politically acceptable and promised to be effective—adjustment of internal demand, tapping international credit sources to finance the deficit or revaluation. A matching set of options were presented to the chronically surplus country. (A characteristic of the Bretton Woods system was that it placed the main burden of adjustment on deficit countries—as if deficits were the wages of monetary sin that should carry political odium.)

The choice of measures had to consider not only the technical merits of each, or a mix of them, for restoring payments equilibrium, but also the differential effects they might be expected to have on domestic sectors and groups as the resulting changes ramify through the national economy. Not surprisingly, a feature of the postwar era (and one that distinguishes it from the interwar period) was the extreme reluctance of deficit countries to undertake austerity programs that classically have been seen as the strong medicine needed to firm up a weak currency. To deflate for the sake of exchange stability runs against the grain of today's welfare-minded societies. Governments on the whole prefer to avail themselves of the multiple opportunities that have been created for short or long term financing of deficits or, increasingly, to take the route of devaluation. On this count there is a discernible difference in the attitudes of Treasury and central bank officials, the latter being more inclined toward the orthodox prescription of domestic retrenchment. This is logical enough. Their primary commitment is to sound money, not growth. They can look with relative equanimity on the deflationary consequences of that commitment since they are better insulated from the compulsions of the welfare society and personally less susceptible to partisan political considerations. They do not run for office. By contrast, the cabinet minister is unprotected. He stands and acts in full public view, unshielded from a voting populace sensitized to the most nuanced changes in economic conditions and thoroughly uninhibited about pointing out their leaders' failings.

Treasury Secretaries, as well as monetary authorities, are obliged to coordinate policy across national boundaries—even as they glance anxiously over their shoulders at the home front. But their cooperation is less institutionalized and less specifically focused than that of central bank directors. Their consultation embraces a wider spectrum of economic concerns—tariffs and trade, the investment strategies of multinational corporations, resource needs—in addition to capital movements and exchange mechanisms. Further, there often are political and security matters lurking in the background of their discussions—e.g., the costs of maintaining American troops in Europe; the political integration of the European Community. Hence, the scope of the Treasuries' domestic powers and responsibilities correspond to the range of considerations that enter into their assessment of international economic problems and interests. It also follows that, thanks to their authority over national economic policy, the primary power of decision on matters of common concern, including monetary ones, lies with the concert of Treasury Secretaries under political instruction.

The Economic Minister's participation in the wider forum of government policymaking holds out the possibility that as international economic questions come to the fore they will be linked to politicomilitary issues, the traditional subject matter of interstate relations. At moments of controversy within the Atlantic Alliance, the U.S. has not hesitated to remind her allies that they still shelter underneath the American security umbrella. More specifically, any yearning that the West German government might have felt to answer the seductive Gaullist call for a common front to resist Europe's domination by American capital and the tyranny of the dollar standard was stiffled by Bonn's overriding interest in retaining American goodwill and American troops. This is but one obvious example of what is a routine bargaining ploy of governments seeking to improve their chances of achieving a given objective by tying together issues in ways that are to their advantage (whether the matters are closely related objectively or simply linked as a matter of tactical convenience).

Linkage can either facilitate or hinder the resolution of an international problem. It is universally accepted that in associating economic cooperation with collective security and political stability in Western Europe a powerful impetus was given to the Common Market. More recently, the formation of the 'Eurosnake,' fixing the rates of EEC currencies against each other, was pressed because monetary union was seen by some governments as a crucial step toward political unity. Equally, there are instances where linkage has had the reverse effect of complicating problems or derailing attempts at solving them. The French penchant for declaring any proposal for concerting monetary policies (or most other policies for that matter) a test of her partners' willingness to enlist in a movement to curtail American influence has alienated her fellow Europeans and hampered constructive planning.

POLITICIZATION

The undeniable importance of most international monetary problems for domestic well-being (as well as for world power relationships), and the sensitive awareness to its effects, if not always its causes, assures that they run a good chance of being 'politicized.' In the common usage of political economists, politicization means an increase in conflict and the shifting of an issue to higher levels of government. The two are usually coupled. Central policymakers—Presidents, Prime Ministers and their cabinets—it is assumed, latch onto a problem only when it cannot be dealt with instrumentally at lower echelons of authority because it affects basic national interests and the structure of interstate relations. Fundamentals have been put in question. Whereas the run-of-the-mill issues can be handled amicably by technical people applying established procedures and practical formulas, those that touch the boundaries of existing agreements open issues about purposes, values and control that demand the arbitration of political authorities.

This formulation seems at once too limited and too formalized. There is reason to question the twin propositions that politics is exclusively about conflict and that the main job of politicians is to manage it. Politics has at least as much to do with fashioning the means to avoid conflict by reconciling interests and with devising instruments for securing the common public interest. It follows that the intervention of central policymaking organs might be necessary to break deadlocks that threaten to erode consensus, to reaffirm a collective purpose or to encourage the inauguration of new arrangements. A problem's politicization entails more than a preoccupation with conflict and domination. It might better be gauged by these three criteria: (1) its perceived *saliency*—for national economic health, for domestic political life, for international relations; (2) its *controversiality*—i.e., the extent and intensity of disagreement in defining its terms and in choosing among options for dealing with it; and (3) the opportunity it is seen as presenting for *winning or losing preferential advantages.*

The hallmark of politicization is an issue's saliency for economic policymaking. The matter at hand might not become the object of partisan conflict and intense public debate, remaining within expert circles and on the financial pages of the newspapers, and yet be politicized. If it bears significantly on the country's prospects for stable economic growth, then almost automatically it will arouse concern for the possible dislocation it threatens and the interests jeopardized, and a careful scrutiny of the utilities and costs of one course of action as opposed to another will be assured. The anticipation of effects that could cause popular anxiety and invite political criticism means that those considerations already are part of the policy process, whether or not the public has as yet been agitated by the issue. To the degree that it is contained within a small circle of interested parties, a greater margin for discretionary governmental judgment is secured—but that margin is restricted nonetheless.

An issue's politicization is also a function of the controversy it evokes—whether that conflict be intragovernmental (among partisan or bureaucratic groupings) or international. Some problems are more critical, more conspicuous and less tractable than others. These traits determine its controversiality. Controversy is usually based on conflicting interests and power rivalries, but it is not always limited to them. Intense controversy often arises over the preferred means to achieve a particular goal, even among those who share interests and agree on primary purposes—e.g., in the monetary field, stability on the exchange markets. These differences can be due to contradictory interpretations of:

1. how economic forces work (Does the "Phillips curve" representing the inverse relationship between unemployment and inflation hold true under all international circumstances? Will floating exchange rates accentuate world inflation through a ratchet effect that shifts price levels upwards? In a free exchange market, would currency speculation stabilize itself?);
2. the motivations of private and public actors (Would the end of fixed exchange rates encourage governments to undertake competitive devaluations? Could the United States be counted on to exercise monetary restraint if the dollar is retained as the prime source of international liquidity? Will export industries in a given country respond to the price stimulus of a devaluation?);
3. the capabilities of government agencies (Can capital and exchange controls be administered with equal reliability and effectiveness by all national banking authorities?);
4. divergent social philosophies (What are the relative weights ascribed one social goal as opposed to another—inflation control versus full employment—in formulating a recommendation? How does one feel about an active, interventionist role for government in regulating economic affairs? Does one place much stock in international institution building as a worthy objective in itself?).

Controversies rooted in different interpretations of reality, the actors' cause-and-effect models of the real world, their values and beliefs, can be every bit as contentious as competition for preferential economic gain or for a position of relative dominance in whatever setup might be under consideration.

Where power rivalries do enter into monetary deliberations (as with the French challenge to the dollar standard, which they saw as enabling the United States to finance its hegemonial global position), and where there is a clear conflict of economic interest (as over the decline in the dollar rate to be expected under a floating rate system), the already technically arduous task of fashioning a new set of viable international agreements is exacerbated. It is equally true that when there is no technically persuasive formula available, the effort to reach a consensus on the terms of an agreement is impeded by a greater readiness to stress the preservation of selfish objectives. Confronted with ambiguous conditions, the focusing of divergent perspectives becomes just as important as the reconciliation of aspirations and interests.

For these reasons, one often detects a tacit understanding among governments that controversy should be kept at a minimum, complications avoided and potential conflict contained by addressing only a problem's manifestations (sanitizing capital flows rather than staunching them at their source). A strictly instrumental approach spares the participants the messy and potentially disruptive business of questioning the system's fundamental assumptions and properties. A constant in the monetary negotiations of the past decade has been the fear that the fragile Humpty-Dumpty of tacit agreements, quiet understandings, customary procedures and complicated compromises that lubricate the awkward system of selective integration might prove hard to put together again once attitudes and commitments are unraveled.

The task, then, of cooperative monetary management facing authorities in the winter of 1973 included these political elements:

1. defining and organizing the collective international purpose;
2. reconciling the different government conceptions of that purpose;
3. agreeing on the preferred means for achieving it while taking account of national economic interests, the intellectual predilections of the several actors and their institutional responsibilities; and
4. fitting any proposal to the domestic political circumstances of governments seen by their populace as custodians of the national welfare.

NOTES TO INTRODUCTION

1. The essential political role of the United States in superintending the postwar economic system, and the implications of its diminished power, are cogently analyzed by Robert Gilpin, "Three Models of the Future," *International Organization* 29, 1 (Winter 1975). The costs and benefits of the American predominance are penetratingly analyzed by Raymond Aron, *The Imperial Republic* (Englewood Cliffs, N.J.: Prentice-Hall, 1974).

2. Among the most insightful examinations of interdependence are: Richard Cooper, *The Economics of Interdependence* (New York: McGraw-Hill, 1967); Richard Cooper, "Economic Interdependence and Foreign Policy in the Seventies," *World Politics* XXIV (January 1972); C. Fred Bergsten, ed., *The Future of the International Economic Order: An Agenda for Research* (Lexington, Mass.: Lexington Books, 1973), especially the contributions by Bergsten and Robert O. Keohane and Joseph S. Nye; Robert Gilpin, "The Politics of Transnational Economic Relations," *International Organization* 29, 1 (Summer 1971); and contributions to the special issue of *International Organization*, "World Politics and International Economics," (Winter 1975).

3. I discuss the influences of domestic welfare politics on the deliberation of international economic problems in "Status Politics and the Emerging International System," *Social Science Information* (Paris) 12, 6 (December 1973).

4. Robert O. Keohane and Joseph S. Nye, "Transgovernmental Relations and International Organizations," *World Politics* XXVI (October 1974). Their concept of transgovernmental activity derives from their more general theory of transnational politics; see Keohane and Nye, eds., *Transnational Relations and World Politics* (Cambridge, Mass.: Harvard University Press, 1972).

5. Keohane and Nye, "Transgovernmental Relations," p. 43.

6. Ibid., p. 44.

7. Ibid., passim.

8. The wellspring of writings on bureaucratic politics is the seminal work of Graham Allison, *The Essence of Decision: Explaining The Cuban Missile Crisis* (Boston: Little, Brown, 1971). See also Morton Halperin's handbook to bureaucratic tactics and strategies, *Bureaucratic Politics and Foreign Policy* (Washington, D.C.: The Brookings Institution, 1974).

9. These networks of consultation and collaboration are discussed by Robert W. Russell, "Transgovernmental Interaction In The International Monetary System, 1960–1972," *International Organization* XX (October 1973).

Chapter 1

The Crisis Unfolds

THE POLICY PROBLEM

The immediate condition demanding attention in February and March of 1973 was the severe dislocations on the exchange markets caused by massive movements of liquid capital that rendered ineffectual the concerted efforts of the central banks to maintain the agreed par values of their currencies. Monetary authorities were being outgunned. The magnitude of the sums involved, their mobility, their skittish sensitivity to speculative triggers, resulted in a classic case of system overload. At the same time, these drastic movements were undermining national monetary policies aimed at controlling strong inflationary pressures which, through their unsettling influence on trade, payments and monetary confidence, were themselves a partial cause of exchange instability.

As a contemporary account chronicled these events, the crisis was ignited when Italy, "bothered by a weakening lira, decided on a two-tier currency market" that threatened holders of large dollar sums [1]. "The ensuing flight of dollars from Italy to Switzerland caused Swiss authorities to float the franc" upward—producing a windfall for those who had sold dollars short and inspiring hopes that other currencies would revalue against the dollar. Six billion dollars of unwanted currency flooded Europe and Japan within a matter of days—the largest portion surging into Germany. The central banks were overwhelmed. With speculation targeted on the dollar (bearish) and the deutschemark (bullish), all efforts on the part of the Federal Reserve Bank in New York and the Deutsche Bundesbank in Frankfurt (with an assist from other collaborating banks) to resist the flow were in vain. The "swap" arrangements that provided central banks with a pool of currency reserves for support operations were outstripped.* What they had not anticipated was the deep erosion of confidence in the dollar; what they could not manage were the great amounts of liquid capital which now were sloshing from country to country.

The speculative waves of February were only temporarily abated by a dollar devaluation and crested early in March as central bank interventions to stem the tide again proved futile. At its height, the German Bundesbank had to absorb $2.7 billion in one twenty-four hour period—a peak that likely would have been surpassed had not authorities felt compelled to close the exchange markets. Fixed par values among the major currencies no longer seemed tenable. The exchanges had proven themselves so vulnerable to drastic capital movements as to hamper normal financial transactions, while rate uncertainty threatened to interfere with international trade. Shutting down the exchanges was an emergency measure to prevent disruption of world commercial and monetary transactions. That closing was a curtain falling on the Bretton Woods system. It was badly damaged, if not entirely swept away, by the speculative tides of March. At the very least, the system's adjustment mechanism** needed a major overhaul. Should it be salvaged and repaired, or replaced; and if drastic alterations were called for, according to what blueprint and with what materials should the job be done?

BACKGROUND

The proximate causes of the speculation were the easiest part of the problem to recognize and to understand. Expansion of mobile capital available for rapid shifts from country to country, currency to currency, reflected the sharp increase in international trade and finance that accompanied the postwar prosperity. Liquidity creation was a logical concomitant to the growth in world economic activity. The largest portion of this liquidity took the form of offshore dollars. For most of the postwar period—until the IMF created Special Draw-

*The "swaps," an American inspiration, had been designed in the mid-1960s as a short term credit source which could be used "to offset private transactions which [were] expected to be limited in duration and reversible, such as large movements of interest-sensitive or speculative short-term capital" [2].

**An adjustment mechanism, as Professor Fritz Machlup explains, is "a systematized method to assure that, when a country's balance of payments slips badly out of line, the country will make the necessary adjustments in its economy or in the exchange rate of its currency—to restore the balance" [3].

ing Rights (SDRs)* to supplement it—the U.S. dollar provided the bulk of international liquidity. As the system's asset medium—i.e., reserve currency, not liable to revaluation—the dollar stood as a fixed standard of value. Confidence in it was confirmed by the knowledge that it could be exchanged, through foreign central banks, into the United States' reserve assets—gold, and later SDRs. The dollar acquired general acceptability in its role as a de facto global currency because it represented a lien on resources anywhere in the world, was backed by the large gold reserves of the U.S. Treasury into which it was convertible (as well as the unchallenged supremacy of the American economy), served as a store of value and had the distinct advantage over gold of bearing interest.

So long as there was confidence in the dollar's unchanging value, and the United States remained committed to convertibility, the net outward flow of dollars (which took the form of overseas investment by American corporations, private bank deposits, and military and tourist expenditures, as well as payments for imported goods and services), dollar creation could continue to serve usefully as the engine for liquidity growth. Faith in that commitment, and thereby in the dollar standard, depended—in the eyes of most private actors, and increasingly for many foreign governments—on the United States' success in offsetting these outflows with large trade surpluses to balance its payments account and to avoid running down its gold assets. As has been commented frequently, there was an unavoidable contradiction between the dollar's role in meeting the system's liquidity needs and the keying of confidence to American payments balances [4]. For U.S. surpluses on the trade account could not fail to reduce the pool of overseas dollars created through deficits on the capital account, and other expenditures. Thus, Robert Triffin neatly summarized the weaknesses of the Bretton Woods system in two phrases: "the creation—or destruction—of world reserves is left at the mercy of unpredictable deficits—or surpluses of the U.S.," and, accordingly, "the U.S. is relieved from any adjustment pressures—and assured . . . of unlimited financing of deficits, whatever their origins, by the currency printing presses of other countries" [5]. The steady erosion of the American surpluses from the late 1950s onwards—swinging into the deficit column a decade later—was the beginning of the system's unraveling.** Convertibility could not be

*SDRs were conceived as an international monetary unit composed of a basket of the leading currencies. At present they are restricted to official credit transactions conducted through the IMF, but they potentially could be made valid for commercial and other financial exchanges as well.

**The postwar monetary system saw sterling as a reserve currency alongside the dollar. The earlier crisis created by Britain's payments deficits and the maintained indefinitely under these circumstances. The monetary system's Achille's heel was about to be revealed.

From another perspective, the problem can be seen as a definitional one involving questionable accounting procedures. Some analysts have suggested that "perhaps the American payments deficit should not have been called a deficit at all. To the extent that the United States provided the world with liquid dollar claims by long-term capital outflows and aid exceeding its current account surplus, it could no more be said to be in deficit than a bank when it makes a loan and enters the dollars on its books" [6]. Actually, as Raymond Vernon has pointed out, "although U.S. gold holdings declined all through the decade of the 1960s, the amount by which total U.S. claims on the rest of the world exceeded the counterclaims continued to rise." What was most disconcerting was that foreigners' claims on the U.S. were in liquid form and might seek convertibility into gold, while the bulk of the U.S. claims were in the form of nonliquid, fixed capital—i.e., American-owned industrial plant. Following this line of reasoning, Vernon concluded that "what the United States has been experiencing . . . is the run on the bank induced largely by the fact that the banker has been insisting, repeatedly, and stridently, that his institution was going bankrupt" [7].

However correct this judgment might be, so long as most individuals and institutions conceptualized the issue in more conventional, if unsophisticated, ways, the contradiction remained. The crisis of confidence in the dollar then was made inevitable by payments deficits, public statements of anxious concern about them and, ultimately, official American attempts to rectify them through changes in the dollar's value. As deficits mounted, outstanding claims on U.S. reserves built up. Between 1969 and 1971, dollar liabilities of the U.S. vis-à-vis foreign official holders rose from $17 billion to $51 billion [9]. Alongside the dollars held as reserves by central banks was the expanding volume of dollars in private accounts which were more liable to seek convertibility or shift into other denominations. (By 1974 the figures had risen dramatically; private and official foreigners together held more than $250 billion in liquid dollar denominated assets, $110 billion as direct claims on the United States) [10].

American deficits were accompanied by a chorus of alarums from government officials, private bankers and academic economists, and veiled discussions of a possible resort to dollar devaluation—all dutifully reported by financial journalists. That prospect engendered a

---

pound's fall from reserve status foreshadowed and accentuated the dollar crisis that followed it in partially overlapping phases [8].

bad case of nerves among large dollar holders. Soon the two began to feed on each other. Signs of a disinclination to hold dollars were taken as evidence of the dangers of continued deficits, while any indications that officials were seriously planning a change in the dollar's status only deepened doubts about its fixed value. Aggravation of the American payments situation in the mid and late 1960s thus had twin effects—both adverse. They rapidly swelled the volume of expatriated dollars (the notorious "dollar overhang") and further weakened confidence in the dollar's stability. Ammunition was being accumulated for speculative campaigns while the chances of its ignition were being enhanced.

The Eurodollar market was the circuit through which the bulk of these external dollars moved. Simply put, it is a system for "accepting deposits and lending in U.S. dollars by banks outside the U.S." [11]. The substantial sums in overseas accounts resulting from corporate investment and net trade deficits had been augmented by the influx of private portfolio investment attracted by the higher rates of interest available during a period of cheap money and easy credit in the U.S.—as well as by the Euromarket's exceptional freedom from the inquisitive eyes of government regulators. From 1969 to 1970 the U.S. capital account shifted, adversely, by a remarkable $12 billion. This massive displacement of personal deposits served at once to plunge the American payments account deeper into the red and to add to the already substantial sums of highly mobile capital ready to move in response to any sign of currency revaluations.

It was during this period that Washington took steps to control and to reduce the hemorrhage of capital. In 1963 it introduced the Interest Equalization Tax intended to dissuade American citizens from shifting bank deposits to take advantage of higher foreign interest rates; set "voluntary" controls on the export of capital in 1965; and, finally, was constrained to impose mandatory controls on foreign direct investment in 1968 (the last mentioned also contained provision for repatriating liquid assets from subsidiaries of American corporations). Despite these increasingly severe attempts at staunching the outflow, net deficits continued to grow. Controls proved administratively inefficient; they could not compensate for other, unregulated forms of foreign spending; and a lax monetary policy (keeping interest rates down to provide easy credit) continued to offer incentive for sending dollars abroad [12]. By 1971 the financial domain of Eurocurrency institutions had expanded to encompass total assets of approximately $125 billion—although exact figures of dollars on deposit outside the U.S. are difficult to pin down [13]. The pyramiding effect of credit expansion by unregulated banks enlarged further the total sum of funds at loose on the money markets.

With the failure of the American campaign to contain capital outflows, dollar devaluation looked more and more like a real possibility in the eyes of potential speculators—i.e., whoever held dollar obligations. The unthinkable was becoming thinkable for private and official actors alike. In Washington, the Nixon administration's initial policy of "benign neglect" was giving way to active concern. Its efforts to seek surcease from deficits through a voluntary agreement on the part of her commercial partners to remove what the U.S. perceived as discriminatory nontariff barriers to trade and upwardly to revalue their currencies against the dollar (thereby improving the terms of trade for U.S. exporters) failed to elicit the desired response. Conventional alternatives were unacceptable. Internal adjustment via a domestic austerity program (curbing money growth, putting up interest rates) not only was politically intolerable at a time when the economy was already stagnating without benefit of outside encouragement, but the orthodox prescription of retrenchment was unlikely to make more than a dent in the trade balance unless it was so severe as to produce an equally undesirable recession. The world economy's dependence on the health of its leading member made everyone hypersensitive to the fine tuning of America's domestic economy and the external effects of any exaggerated dial twisting.

The strains that were building found release in the system's weakest link—the exchange markets. By May 1971 speculation on an upvaluation of the deutschemark vis-à-vis the dollar had reached such proportions that the Bonn government found it expedient to let the mark float freely against other currencies—that is, to permit its exchange rate to be determined by buyers and sellers on the open market rather than maintained within a prescribed band through official support operations. The voracious demand for marks assured that any official defense would be futile. Foreseeing a series of retreats, each of which could only confirm the likelihood of another profitable—for speculators—revaluation, and upset by the inflation of its internal money supply, German authorities cut the mark loose. The German float was the first formal acknowledgment that the par value system was losing its viability. It also inaugurated a period in which floating—free or managed, general or limited, and of varying durations—became a feature of the international monetary system.

The irreparable breach was made a few months later by the dramatic American decision in August 1971, at a moment of extreme pressure, to devalue the dollar and to terminate its convertibility. It was that action that would lead ineluctably to the dislocations and eventual breakdown of March 1973. Desanctification of the dollar through devaluation meant that its value was liable to change through official act just like less exalted currencies; and by "closing the gold window"—i.e., the U.S. no longer would accept dollars and pay for them in gold—the American action obviated the dollar's position as an unchanging standard of value, engendering a pervasive uncertainty and inspiring a general search for a secure, and perhaps profitable, financial haven.

By removing the one fixed reference point for the par value system, the devaluation opened the way to a more volatile exchange market. Shifts in the par values of the leading currencies, which had been exceptional in the earlier postwar years but had become more common as governments felt constrained to respond to larger payments desequilibria, were now a routine feature of monetary life. The inhibitions against recurrent rate changes that had developed out of a strict reading of the IMF regulations were almost entirely removed with the American action. As revaluations became accepted as normal, so was currency speculation ensconced within the system. The proximate cause triggering a particular surge could be any one of several: a sharp (or prolonged) imbalance in a country's trade and/or payments accounts; a widening of interest rate spreads; domestic economic performance—signs of overheating, signs of a downturn (this latter if you were not too literal in your reading of economic theory); rumors of impending revaluations; reports of actions—actual, intended or imagined—by large financial institutions or multinational firms. The participants were equally numerous: calculating financial operators gambling on the exchange markets; the prudent treasurers of commercial enterprises protecting assets by hedging against rate changes; or exchange directors of international banks anticipating currency developments (and occasionally giving them a push in a preferred direction). Whatever the mix of motives and catalysts, the overriding reality was the constant threat of bandwagon movements unresponsive to central bank proclamations and interventions.

On a large enough scale, these movements could force a rate change already under consideration—or even dictate one that had not been contemplated. Moreover, there was no risk to the 'speculator,' since official interventions in defense of par values meant that monetary authorities would buy or sell at a fixed rate. If the expected revaluation occurred, the dealer who had sold short and bought long picked up the difference between the old and new rate; if revaluation was resisted successfully, then the dealer incurred only small transaction costs. Hence the famous "one way bet." Anticipating these changes and forecasting events which could set them off logically became the vocation of the foreign exchange departments in international banks, of exchange directors in the great multinationals, of commercial traders and investors, and of any other potential dealer in foreign currencies whose position either offered the opportunity for gain or made him vulnerable to losses from being caught on the wrong side of a revaluation. Under these circumstances, it is only an arbitrary judgment that can draw a clear line between the pure speculator—whose dealings on the exchange markets are unrelated to any substantial, 'legitimate' trade or investment interest—and someone who is defensively protecting a stake—e.g., the trader covering himself through the forward market and estimating "leads" and "lags" or the business concern deciding in what currencies to denominate its operating capital [14]. Whatever the analytical challenge of providing a crisp definition of the speculator, there was no gainsaying the practical danger associated with the presence of large pools of mobile capital that could be stirred into irresistable movements for or against currencies suspected of revaluation.

The period from the ending of dollar convertibility in August 1971 to the crisis of February-March 1973 was a transition phase between the by then suspect—if not yet wholly discredited—system of fixed rates and some still undefined replacement. Uncertainty was its trademark, and a sense of impending crisis its dominant mood. Major governments sought unsuccessfully to repair the rents that had been torn in the fabric of international monetary relations through a patchwork of expediencies and remedial adjustments; numerous proposals for more basic reform were broached in the several forums that exist for that purpose; and the position of monetary authorities striving to maintain a modicum of exchange stability became increasingly tenuous. The more far-reaching reform effort unfolded in multiple meetings and assemblies—Working Party 3 of the OECD's Economic Policy Committee, central bankers at the Bank for International Settlements, and the IMF's Group of Ten leading financial and trading nations (later to be partially superseded by the Committee of Twenty on Reform of the International Monetary System). Their attention centered on, and the deliberations aimed at, reaching agreement on the fundamental issues that had bedeviled monetary officials for a decade: questions of liquidity (the optimal level of reserves, and the form they should take); the distribution of reserves; adjustment procedures and mechanisms; and convertibility (especially, how to handle the huge dollar overhang).

As of the winter of 1973 the record was spotty. Some notable progress toward renovation had been made, but no accord was in prospect on the fundamental question of the vulnerable, and increasingly unsteady, dollar standard. So long as the U.S. shyed away from relinquishing the privileges of its position (and her economic partners lacked both the unity and the persuasive formula to press for an agreed alternative), no basic resolution was forthcoming. The one outstanding success was the conclusion of the protracted negotiations (under IMF auspices and dating back to the 1960s) to create the rudimentary international money—SDRs. At the outset, though, SRDs were viewed as a supplement to the dollar rather than its replacement as the reserve currency. Indeed, the idea had the backing of the U.S., which saw SDRs as an additional asset medium, augmenting reserves, that could help cover American deficits. Europeans, for their part, saw in the formation of SDRs a partial first step toward relieving the dollar of its reserve function and a potential instrument for freeing liquidity creation from its dependence on American deficits. The eventual accord took the form of a compromise wherein the Europeans gave their agreement in exchange for greater voting power in the IMF, bringing to an end the United States' power to control the organization's policy.

The SDR initiative, however positive, was but a tentative move in the direction of structural reform of the world's monetary system. Little progress had been made either in forging a consensus on the shape of an overall reform strategy or in preparing contingency plans for responding to the inevitable, and expected, upheavals on the currency markets.

The immediate effort after the dollar devaluation of August 1971 had been centered on repegging the major currencies and enhancing the chances for maintaining them by restoring payments equilibrium. In December, at the now memorable monetary summit at the Smithsonian in Washington, the United States, led by the calculatingly blunt and abrasive Secretary of the Treasury, John Connally, painfully extracted an agreement for a revaluation of 8 percent by the other major currencies against the dollar.* The goal was a massive shift in trade—a report of the President's Council of Economic Advisers argued for a 'turnaround' figure of $13 billion [15]. If the proposed rate changes could generate an improvement in the American trade balance on anything like that scale, the realignment would go

*Eight percent was the average. The revaluation of the deutschemark, for example, was 12 percent. The emphasis was placed on an upvaluation by the Europeans and Japanese, rather than an American devaluation, for three reasons: the U.S. wanted collective sanction for a reordering of rates (in part to ward off countervailing action by other governments); there was an element of face still involved in a devaluation which retained some of its stigma of monetary fecklessness; and American law requiring Congressional approval of any revaluation promised a time delay in implementation.

a long way toward establishing a viable rate structure, and with it general monetary stability. That, at least, was the American game plan. In this optimistic frame of mind, the administration moved to dismantle the picket fence of capital controls which had been built, with dubious results, to curb outflows. The muted optimism voiced by conference participants could not conceal doubts that the battery of revaluations they had just concluded were only a finger in the dike holding back American deficits, rather than a scheme that addressed the underlying faults of the system. The Smithsonian notwithstanding, world reserves were still a function of the U.S. balance of payments performance; and there still was no restriction on the financing of American deficits.

The short term bet that balance would be restored to payments accounts, and with it a return of confidence in the dollar, turned out to be a losing proposition. None of these objectives was achieved. U.S. exports responded with disappointing sluggishness to the tonic. Whether this performance was simply in keeping with the J-curve lag familiar to economic analysts, or because trade elasticities had been overestimated or prices were less responsive to exchange rate changes than had been assumed, there was no dramatic surge of exports or visible improvement in the balance of trade. On the capital markets, the predicted reflux of dollars back to the U.S. never materialized. Nothing really had happened to force a turn in the movement of speculative funds. Retrospectively, it seems that large scale capital moves are keyed to long term swings of exchange rates and that those swings cannot be reversed by cosmetic gestures. The "cure" administered to the dollar at the Smithsonian promised little—and delivered less—to shift the tide running against the dollar. A pronounced preference among currency holders for marks and against dollars had taken root on the exchange markets, assuring that any event favorable to the latter (higher interest rates or a return to a trade surplus, neither of which in fact took place) would be understated, while those favorable to the mark would be accentuated.

This questionable strategy of predicating a restoration of monetary health on a renewed American trade surplus received no assist from the United States' trading partners. Fearful of competition from presumably advantaged American goods, some succumbed to the mercantalist temptation of neutralizing the effect of the revaluations through various strategems. The year following the Smithsonian agreement was notable for the array of imaginative devices by which commercial rivals tried to erode the exchange advantage that had been conceded. Japan, with the yen under constant upward pressure, strove to reduce its movement by ingenious subterfuges entailing the camouflage of reserves and veiled export subsidies. Most sensitive about a threat to Japan's trade position, Japanese authorities were prepared for a covert commercial struggle. The French resorted to the expediency of a two-tiered rate system—the separation of the commercial from the financial franc—permitting them to maintain the lower rate in the commercial category while preserving the worth of its currency for other purposes. The strong conviction held at the Treasury and the White House, exaggerated but with some basis in truth, that the United States had been denied the fruits of the dollar devaluation so arduously won was to color American thinking subsequently and to influence the American attitude toward flexible exchange rates.

The unexpectedly slow improvement in the U.S. trade account meant that there was only a slight restoration of confidence in the dollar and the nervous exchange markets were never fully calmed. Within a few months, in May 1972, renewed heavy buying of the deutschemark led German authorities once again to refloat upward—a move that, while apparently further favoring the American trade position, was more significant as an indicator that the hope of reestablishing monetary stability was not being realized. Another blow was dealt the new rate alignment when the pound, again in trouble, was taken off its peg in June 1972 and allowed to float—in its case downward. By pieces, and by degrees, the jerrybuilt renovation undertaken at the Smithsonian was crumbling. The only changes in the underlying conditions that had provoked the paralyzing speculation of 1971 were ones that increased the destructive potential of the forces at work. The mutability of the dollar standard had been recognized in official act, payments equilibrium remained an elusive goal, the dollar overhang had been enlarged by continued American deficits and the multiplier effect of the Eurocurrency markets, and the vulnerability of monetary authorities was reconfirmed by the more frequent resort to floating. For government officials the period was an interregnum in which each of the leading powers sought to protect its main interest—a favorable trade position, freedom for domestic monetary policy, protection against disruptive capital inflows—while preserving the formal structure of cooperation. As Jeremy Morse, chairman of the Committee of Twenty, was led to reflect, "in difficult times when the scaffolding of a centrally beneficial system appears weakened, nations pay more regard to their self-interest and try to preserve their freedom to act in that self-interest" [16]. Even measures of defensive mercantalism met with little success in protecting governments against the consequences of a system failure. Not only had events largely removed control from the hands of individual governments, but developments also were overwhelming their collective capacity to deploy effectively the powers at their common disposal. At stake was the infrastructure of international economic activity and all that depended on it. The collective purpose had to be reasserted, and its instruments redesigned.

The Winter Crisis

As with most terminal diseases, the end was predictable, yet still surprisingly swift when it came. By early February 1973 the symptoms of grave illness, familiar to all those ministering to the patient from previous crises, took on a fatal appearance. First, the resistance of the chronic American deficit to the curative of devaluation; pessimistic advisories about the chances of recovery; and the feverish flight from the dollar—the waves of hot money sweeping into Germany and Switzerland and swamping official rescue efforts. In a belated attempt at resuscitation, the U.S. devalued the dollar a second time in the vain hope of stabilizing its condition. It was an action contrary to the administration's expressed intentions, stated out of belief in the resiliency of American exports, and in encouragement of new steps by the surplus countries. What eighteen months earlier was a dramatic, epochal initiative, this time around had all the earmarks of a despairing gesture.

After a brief respite of only a few days, speculative runs started up again—as if the appetites of speculators had only been whetted by the 6 percent devaluation and the worst fears of defensive sellers confirmed. The ephemeralness of the relief, the seeming imperviousness of the market to the conventional prods and cues, stunned both government officials and private commentators. Official credibility had been damaged beyond repair by the years of temporizing and expedient adjustment. The movement of relatively small sums could stampede hordes of anxious dollar holders. By the first week in March, disorder reigned on the exchange markets. "Unprecedented" proclaimed *The Times* of London [17]; "incomprehensible" admitted *Le Monde* [18]—giving journalistic statement to the shocked reaction felt in official circles.

THE ANALYTICAL PROBLEM: ADVERSITY AND THE DECISION PROCESS

In adversity the initial reaction normally is avoidance. Dangers are denied, the seriousness of the situation underplayed, the event of the moment is read to conform with experience and to confirm orthodox remedies, and reiterated faith in established policies substitutes for direct confrontation of root causes [19]. For the academic observor and commentator, it is the occasion to restate one's pet ideas, to reaffirm the cogent insights of one's preferred formulas and theories. Preserving the integrity of one's model of reality is a priority concern of officials and theorists alike.

In most instances, government behavior is in keeping with the parsimony principle. When faced with adversity, the inability to achieve goals and to fulfill expectations doing what one has been doing, there is a strong propensity to deal with the situation at minimal intellectual cost (change in one's belief system and values) and with least disturbance of established procedures or challenge to prevailing interests—be they economic, bureaucratic or professional. Thus the readily identifiable tendency to define a problem specifically and narrowly and to address it incrementally. In a recent treatise on cognitive processes and decisionmaking, John Steinbruner demonstrates how an "analytical model" of decisionmaking with its assumptions of systematically logical problem solving is peculiarly inappropriate when applied to government leaders in times of change. On those occasions, Steinbruner argues, the evident complexity of the problems; the multiple and contradictory values presented; the shifting field of actors; the imperfect information; and, perhaps most important, internationally, the dispersion of authority among countries (and among government agencies) militate strongly against the critical scrutiny of premises and purposes on which innovation depends. The thinking of Steinbruner's "cybernetic actor" is characterized by an overriding need to simplify an incomprehensively complex world—"uncertainty control" as it is called. He does so "by focussing on a few incomplete variables, by eliminating any serious calculation of probable outcomes. . . . The decision-maker is assumed to have a small set of responses and decision rules which determine the course of action to take once he has received information to which he is sensitive" [20]. A key issue in comparing the response of officials in different institutional roles is their ability to depart from this pragmatic logic, the factors that induce them to do so and the direction any conjectured innovation takes.

The breakdown of the exchange markets, with its promise of disrupting all manner of commerce and finance, was too obviously dangerous to permit the full luxury of avoidance behavior. Some kind of response to restore order, jointly undertaken, was imperative if the world economy was not gradually to wind down. The form of that response, though, its scope, who would initiate it, and the precise role of the several national and bureaucratic actors in the play was less evident. Different approaches were liable to have profoundly different consequences, not only for the chances of restabilizing the exchange markets but also for the medley of underlying, interlocking monetary conditions that were cause and effect of these recurrent exchange crises. The strategy pursued also would have serious implications for national policymaking and the powers of those officials in the central banks and Treasuries immediately responsible for implementing whatever arrangements would be agreed upon.

The Decision Process

The most critical stage in the decision process is that of setting its terms. The way one defines the problem often indicates the answer. It certainly controls the range of alternatives considered. What goes into an official's formulation of an issue and assessment of a situation? One of the stickiest problems for the policy analyst is to accord proper place in his theory, or in his explanation of a given event, to both the institutional factors that influence official behavior and the individual's own processes of thought, deliberation and choice. It is no easy chore to separate the two sources of behavior and to delineate the several considerations that come together to determine an official's thinking. It is especially difficult in a complex government setting. While there is a formal hierarchy of authority, only rarely are the subordinate agencies orchestrated by a chief executive to achieve centrally defined goals. Ideas and opinions do not openly confront each other, to be synthesized in a clearly enunciated position. Rather there is an elaborate, and usually ragged, interaction among numerous players simultaneously refining the ends while arguing over preferred means. Moreover, official thinking at all levels is most often lacking in the precision and consistency that allows one to discern and represent it.

One way of bringing the institutional and behavioral facets together is to concentrate on the individual decisionmaker (wherever he is located in government) who serves as the analytical focus, while considering the multiple influences—of whatever origin—that have a bearing on his attitudes and conduct—that is, his manner of viewing the problem, formulating options, and weighing the values they incorporate and the choices to be made. In this way, no a priori primacy is given either to the conditioning effect of organizations or system-defined national interests *or* to the ideas, proclivities and personality of the individual actor. It also should enable the analyst to avoid making artificial and arbitrary distinctions between interests and values, prematurely according priority to one or the other. Rather, this approach assumes an affinity of interests (economic; bureaucratic—national or international; professional) with values (models, doctrines, philosophies, academic theories.).

It is useful to outline those *predisposing factors* at work in influencing officials as they address international monetary issues. Without elaborating each, or indicating here how proximate they were to the point of decision, their denotation nonetheless provides a schematic representation of the various intersecting forces.

I. General National Attitudes
Reflective of

A. Size

small countries—being more vulnerable to international developments, they must keep their eye on system performance and incline toward precise rules of behavior

big countries—by virtue of their relative insularity, they have greater latitude in pursuing national ends and tolerance for different monetary regimes

B. National Experience

France and Japan—out of a tradition of cultural nationalism stress the zero-sum part of the game

Germany—stresses the nonzero-sum aspect as a reaction to the Nazi past; Weimar inflation as a strong negative reference point

United Kingdom—a residual sense of global responsibility diminished by the experience of recurrent devaluations; mass unemployment of the 1930s as a strong negative reference point

C. Economic Circumstance—Primary Concerns

United States—threat to the dollar standard; need for reserve expansion, easy adjustment; maintain nonconvertibility

Germany—stem capital movements; control liquidity growth

France—maintain export position; avoid dollar devaluation

D. Philosophical or Doctrinal Preferences

Germany—principled commitment to the free market concept; dislike for state controls (as on capital movements)

France—confidence in administered solutions to economic problems

The Netherlands—internationalism as enlightened self-interest

E. International Commitments and Mutual Obligations

F. Security Interests and Global Ambitions

II. Bureaucratic-Organizational-Professional (Central Banks)

A. Preservation of Unique Missions
intervention on the exchange markets to maintain par values

B. Enabling of Economic Management Functions
regulate capital movements to permit control over domestic money supply

C. Institutional Powers, Legal Status and Relations to Political Authorities
the Banque de France's dependence
the Deutsche Bundesbank's relative independence

D. Customary Procedures and Conventions

E. International Commitments and Mutual Obligations

III. Individual

A. System-Defined Responsibilities
B. Personal Interpretation of National Interests
C. Conditioning of Institutional Role
D. Education, Training and Professional Background
E. Critical Experiences
F. Exchanges with Nongovernment Experts
G. Interpersonal Ties with Domestic Colleagues
H. Interpersonal Ties with Central Bank Counterparts

This checklist of the many ingredients which go into a policymaker's belief system and help shape his attitude set does not say anything specific about the ways in which they combine or what the consequences are for handling a problem of interdependence. It does highlight the array of factors that are at work when governments set about the task of making national policy on a sensitive international economic issue. Bearing them in mind, let us look back at our earlier questions of who is most inclined to take an aggregate, internationalist view of monetary issues, and which circumstances are most suited to positive efforts at extending collaborative management.

Earlier we suggested a number of keys to assessing (1) the likelihood that a particular official will press for a system-oriented policy, and (2) the potential that a given situation has for pushing solutions in that direction. With regard to the former issue, we stressed the institutional role. It was conjectured that officials in the central banks who have had concrete responsibilities for monetary management requiring active cooperation with their colleagues in other governments are most likely to give a prominent place to the implications of any proposal for established rules of international conduct and stable interstate exchanges. Since they are constantly exposed to the views of other governments (as well as those of international bureaucrats), they are perhaps more accustomed to look at problems from the standpoint of overall system need; their collegiality could encourage ways of defining organizational missions that place premiums on international networks of cooperation; and, consequently, they might tend to expand their view of the situation to embrace the broad interplay of world economic forces.

The complementary hypothesis is that as participants in transgovernmental consultative networks they would favor, and perhaps actively campaign for, relatively wide-ranging plans to design new instruments of cooperative management—e.g., to regulate capital flows and exchange market operations, to apply prescriptive rules for rate adjustments or to formalize harmonization of domestic monetary policies. These straightforward hypotheses, which would appear to follow logically from the theory of interdependent policymaking, are based on two suppositions. One is that the officials most directly engaged in these networks—central bankers—are predisposed by virtue of this involvement, and the distinctive outlook associated with that role, to look with special sympathy on a collective response that deepens intergovernmental coordination. To carry it one step further, the inference is that this concern for the nonzero-sum part of the game might even point to expanded powers for extranational institutions. The second is that in a crisis situation that opens the possibility for major structural reforms, an initiating role is accorded officials already engaged in transgovernmental coordination.

Both of these assumptions are open to qualification and amendment, and the hypotheses based on them suggest counterhypotheses. Taking the latter proposition first, the presumed latitude for central bank initiative is contrary to the tendency for higher political authority to take command of policy in crisis situations. The more critical the problem, the greater the incentive for central direction and oversight. Whereas in conducting comparatively routine operations monetary authorities act relatively free of political supervision, within the guidelines of existing policy, increased saliency brings into play cabinet officers. Ministers have political constituencies and are sensitive to the implications for domestic economic welfare and management. They also are concerned with their nation's security and foreign policy goals. The resulting politicization means greater attentiveness to the domestic and global effects of any turn of monetary events and to any change in the customary manner of dealing with them.

That self-consciousness about the broader ends and purposes of national policy might be either a plus or minus for the deepening of international cooperation. In one sense, central leadership will be less "internationalist"—i.e., anxious about relinquishing the instruments of domestic policy and mercantile in its defense of short term national interests threatened by the crisis. For this reason, it might be expected that cabinet ministers will seek to limit consideration of far-reaching structural innovations and to impose this approach on officials with more technical responsibilities and/or internationalist orientations. From another perspective, though, the intervention of political authorities can have the salutary effect of giving impetus to efforts at forging new cooperative arrangements.

The other proposition incorporated into speculative theories about the influence of transgovernmental groupings of monetary officials speaks to their motivation. It postulates an inclination on the part of monetary authorities to build new structures on the foundation of existing cooperative arrangements. It assumes that officials whose organizational roles are defined at least partly in international terms exhibit an intellectual predilection for international answers to outstanding problems. Questions must be raised first, though, as to the notion of "international" we have in mind. Do we speak of an institutionalized, superintending monetary agency (an enhanced IMF) with powers of autonomous decision *or* merely of strengthening and extending the range of intergovernmental consultation *or* does one view the international economy as a functional entity and visualize an approach that devolves "authority" onto a free market mechanism, as would be the case if there were a genuine free float of currencies? For it is possible to diminish national powers without increasing those of extranational bodies. Each of these conceptions has quite different implications for the status and power of national monetary authorities that might or might not be in keeping with their present image of their own role.

Second, this projection of officials' attitudes toward policy innovation from existing arrangements runs the risk of too casually attributing to central bankers a technocrat's architectonic impulse, which will lead them—if left unhampered—to construct brave new institutions, in whatever domain they find themselves, in response to whatever problem they confront. Any such assumption is an exaggeration, if not an outright distortion, of their actual attitudes. Not only is it more reasonable to expect a larger measure of procedural conservatism, but the above notion also overlooks the fact that central bankers might be averse to planning new cooperative facilities as much for the threat such innovation would pose to their existing powers, which remain nationally based and nationally oriented, as for the practical and political difficulties of proceeding with elaborate initiatives.

Such hypothetical issues on which governmental actors can be expected to impede or advance monetary collaboration in a crisis situation point to both the range of power they enjoy and the scope of their intellectual and policy concern. Which of these assumptions and propositions best represent the reality of international monetary policymaking should be revealed in reviewing the actions taken by the principle governments involved in the exchange crisis.

NOTES TO CHAPTER 1

1. *The New York Times*, March 17, 1973. A detailed account is provided by Sidney E. Rolfe and James I. Burtle, *The Great Wheel: The World Monetary System* (New York: Quadrangle, 1973), pp. 114–115.

2. Richard Cooper *The Economics of Interdependence* (New York: Mc-Graw-Hill, 1967), p. 48.

3. *The New York Times*, September 14, 1975.

4. An excellent analysis of this problem is presented in Benjamin J. Cohen, "Major Issues of World Monetary Reform" (Prepared for The Commission on Critical Choices for Americans, August 1974).

5. *The Smithsonian Agreement and Its Aftermath* (New York: Council On Foreign Relations, 1972), p. 50.

6. Hans O. Schmitt, "The International Monetary System," *International Affairs* 50, 2 (April 1974): 196. The same point has been made by Raymond Vernon, *The Economic Environment of International Business* (Englewood Cliffs, N.J.: Prentice-Hall, 1972), p. 9.

7. Raymond Vernon, "A Skeptic Looks At The Balance of Payments," *Foreign Policy*, no.4 (Fall 1971).

8. An excellent historical account is Richard N. Gardner, *Sterling-Dollar Diplomacy*, 2nd ed. (New York: The Clarendon Press, 1972).

9. Noted by Dr. Otmar Emminger in *The Smithsonian Agreement*, p. 51.

10. Estimate by Marina vN. Whitman in "Leadership Without Hegemony," *Foreign Policy*, no. 20 (Fall 1975).

11. Cooper, p. 117.

12. For a discussion of developments during this period see Rolfe and Burtle, pt. II.

13. The annual report of the Bank for International Settlements calculates the volume of funds in Eurocurrency institutions. Judgments differ, though, as to their precision and as to the importance of the velocity of capital on these markets. For a review of Eurobanking, see Geoffrey Bell, *The Euro-Dollar Market and the International Financial System* (New York: Halsted Press, 1973), and Jane Seddon Little, *Euro-Dollars* (N.Y.: Harper & Row, 1975).

14. The technical definition of speculation offered by Professor Ronald I. McKinnon of Stanford defines it simply as "The purchase of one currency for

another (forward or spot) in order to hold an open position through time in anticipation of a favorable change in relative currency prices." "Floating Foreign Exchange Rates 1971–1974: The Emporer's New Clothes" (Paper presented to the Carnegie-Mellon/Rochester University Monetary Conference, November 15, 1974), p. 16.

15. *Economic Report of the President 1971* Council of Economic Advisors (Washington, D.C.: U.S. Government Printing Office).

16. C.J. Morse, Speech to the International Monetary Conference, "The Evolving Monetary System," Williamsburg, Virginia, June 7, 1974.

17. *The Times* of London, March 4, 1973.

18. *Le Monde*, March 3, 1973.

19. The classic work on the psychology of decisionmaking under stress is Leon Festinger, *Conflict, Decision and Dissonance* (Palo Alto: Stanford University Press, 1964). I made a tentative attempt at applying these ideas to governmental policy in "The Problem of Innovation and the Nixon-Kissinger Foreign Policy," *International Studies Quarterly* 17, 3 (September 1973).

20. John Steinbruner, *The Cybernetic Theory of Decision* (Princeton, N.J.: Princeton University Press, 1974).

Chapter 2

Crisis Management

The government authorities charged with reconstituting the exchange system could readily agree as to the immediate problem and its proximate causes—the loss of confidence in certain currencies, massive shifts of speculative capital, the impotence of the central banks to contain them. All parties were in accord as well that this phenomenon was only the vivid and most obvious manifestation of deeper conditions. However, according to how large a slice of reality one included in the analysis, and the judgments made about the factors at work, the overall situation could appear quite differently.

Any formulation of the problem, whether by a central bank director, Treasury Secretary, head of government or, for that matter, academic economist, can be measured along three axes. There are (1) a temporal dimension: Is the focus on the immediate source of disturbance or does it look back for underlying causes and look ahead to consider requirements for, and threats to, stable performance in the future? (2) a latitudinal dimension: How many facets of international and domestic life is it thought necessary and appropriate to incorporate into the problem's exposition? and (3) a social dimension: In assessing causes, and desired effects, how much attention is paid political, administrative and social concerns?

Depending on one's perspective, the "problem" conceivably was any or all of the following—the declining confidence in the dollar; therefore, the 1971 devaluation; therefore, the chronic American payments deficits; therefore, reckless monetary and fiscal policies that fueled domestic inflation in the U.S., and/or the excessive rigidity in the par value system that did not permit more frequent and smaller rate changes that would allow for necessary adjustments in a noncrisis atmosphere, and/or the awkward and irregular procedures for liquidity creation, and/or the need to replace the dollar with a composite reserve currency, and/or excessive liquidity that enables the U.S. and other deficit countries to run recurrent deficits, and/or the extremely high level of American capital investment abroad; thus, the "exorbitant privilege" accorded the U.S. dollar; thus, the need for stricter convertibility procedures *or* a more flexible adjustment mechanism; and/or uncontrolled growth of liquid capital in the hands of noninstitutional actors and its unregulated movement across national frontiers; and/or the weakness of capital controls.

Expanding the definition of the "problem" along the social axis, it encompasses the ultrasensitivity of governments to group pressures for rapid increases in disposible income and the consequent unwillingness to accept austerity measures when dictated by constant external deficits; and/or the high rates of inflation in certain key countries resulting from these indulgent policies; and/or the weakness of Treasuries and central banks in exercising their authority to regulate the financial markets and the political philosophies that make them hesitant about doing so; and/or the dilatoriness of national monetary authorities in responding to signs of payments disequilibria and taking preemptive action—internally or along the adjustment avenue; and/or America's global security commitments, the failure of her allies to defray a proper portion of the costs, and/or the U.S.'s extravagent and ill-considered engagements in areas peripheral to Western security.

Each of these numerous elements, in various combinations with the others, could be found in official analyses and expert interpretations of the exchange crisis. By implication, then, the first question facing economic officials was whether to treat root causes. Should they attempt to reach a consensus on the situation's full dimensions (or at least some significant portion of them), and try to develop a package of reforms that would link measures for shoring up the exchange markets to a more fundamental renovation of the international monetary system, *or*, rather, limit themselves to remedial steps. There was a strong initial feeling that their efforts should be carefully delimited. The pressures of crisis management normally do not permit contemplation of the global state of affairs or negotiation of a complicated agreement. In the first weeks of the crisis, as speculative pressures mounted, no national official of rank voiced the expectation that the collapse of the fixed rate system would evoke that sense of communality which would facilitate setting an agenda, much less elicit a joint plan of action. The recurrent deliberations during the preceeding years had done their job too well in highlighting the obstacles to accord.

The general disposition to search for expediences does not mean that the broader implications went entirely unnoticed. Governments' recommendations for meeting the crisis, and their tactical maneuvering to secure preferred solutions, were designed in cognizance of how their own national interests would be affected. They were equally sensitive to how any short term expedient could slant later negotiations on more far-reaching changes. Crisis behavior clarifies, rather than obscures, a government's underlying thinking and purposes. The fact that policymakers find themselves responding to events whose occurrence they neither desired nor truly anticipated can afford a better insight into official attitudes for that very reason. Nothing is as revealing as judgments made in haste and decisions taken under the press of events.

A second characteristic of the early response was the rapid involvement of central policymaking bodies. At first the problem had appeared on the periphery of their attention. A world that had grown accustomed to chronic payments problems, and jaded about exchange market tensions, relegated this latest perturbance to the financial pages of the newspapers and left it to the care of the central banks. However, as the capital flows accelerated and grew into a massive tide, tension became crisis, emblazoned in front page headlines, and soon the preoccupation of Treasury Secretaries and heads of government. Once having grown to such proportions as to force a second dollar devaluation, the monetary situation was the abiding concern of the highest public officials. Central bank directors and their senior deputies continued to be prominent players and had a hand in fashioning the strategy for restoration and reform. But they now were participants in an exercise of crisis management wherein the power of ultimate decision, and, in most instances, the prerogative of policy initiation, had been taken by their political superiors.

The pattern of response also saw an accentuation of positions taken previously. Interpretations of what was happening reiterated the well-established views of government actors, and the initial proposals for salvaging the situation strongly reflected these perceptions. Reactions were keyed by that medley of predisposing factors that each participant brought to the crisis and that served as the touchstones of responsive behavior—general, system-defined conceptions of the national and international interest; bureaucratic or organizational responsibilities; and individual philosophies and proclivities that are at once personal adaptations of institutional influences and independent interpretations of them. They are the cognitive lodestones according to which a map of international economic life is composed and in reference to which an official navigates.

NATIONAL POSITIONS

Now let us turn our attention to the major governments involved in the exchange crisis and examine how each approached it. Their review and analysis should illuminate the process whereby national policymaking is brought to bear on a problem of common concern.

Germany

The Federal Republic had been at the center of the monetary storm. Her impressive export performance and large trade surpluses, restrained monetary policies and low rate of inflation, made the deutschemark uniquely attractive for those seeking a stable (and potentially rewarding) financial harbor. With the mark the recipient of the attentions of the speculators, the Deutsche Bundesbank had been in the forefront of the central banks' unsuccessful campaign to maintain exchange stability. Between January and March 1973, the German banking system absorbed $12 billion in capital inflows. Thanks to its abortive purchase of dollars, the devaluation of February left the Bundesbank with a loss of $2 billion—a sum that surpassed the losses of August 1971, and was itself to be exceeded in March. However substantial, these losses were minor compared to the disruptive effects on domestic economic management. The huge influx had worked havoc on the country's monetary policies, which were aimed at contracting credit as part of Bonn's anti-inflation strategy. No such policy had a chance in the face of these enormous external intrusions. For governments to lose collective control over the exchange markets was for each to lose individual control over domestic monetary policy. In German eyes, as Bundesbank Deputy-Governor Dr. Otmar Emminger declared a few months later, "The previous [exchange] regime did not break down because of the unrest on the exchange markets, [but] because of its inflationary implications" [1].

Inflation has stood as the negative reference point for German economic policy throughout the postwar recovery and prosperity, a collective memory of the searing experience of Weimar. It has been an equally prominent consideration coloring their attitude toward international monetary issues. It is the prevailing German belief that stability in both realms depends above all on successfully resisting the forces of inflation and protecting the world economy from its corrosive effects. In recent years, according to this view, monetary authorities have been remiss in their overly tolerant acceptance of inflationary tendencies which were transmitted through, and compounded by, two features of the international monetary system—its generous provision of credit facilities and its readiness to force revaluation on those countries that succeeded in containing the spiral of costs and prices.

The main culprit was the United States, abusing its privileges as the world's banker. Washington, it was felt, had improvidently expanded the money supply in the mid and late sixties to cover the costs of the Vietnam War. The Johnson Administration's commitment to both guns and butter translated into low interest rates; an excessive increase in credit, demand and cost pressures; and, with them, large overseas trade deficits. The inflationary consequences were multiple. American goods became increasingly uncompetitive under the press of rises in domestic costs, exacerbating the strain on the American trade balance. Fear of inflation, low interest rates and general monetary uncertainty in the U.S. also gave renewed impetus to capital outflows already attracted abroad by investment opportunities. In this way, a large share of the excess liquidity created in the U.S. found its way onto the Eurocurrency markets, where it had the dual effect of fanning inflationary embers in Europe and adding to the pool of mobile capital. Since the mark was the continent's strongest currency, and the one most liable to upward revaluation, it was inevitable that the biggest share of this surplus should wind up in Germany. Given the inordinate difficulties of controlling the Eurocurrency markets, the Bonn government saw itself as prey to forces beyond its control.

Part of the blame, as we mentioned, lay with the international monetary structure. In being too solicitous to deficit countries by providing generously for deficit financing (through the IMF and General Agreement to Borrow), it slackened the pressure on governments to exercise the internal discipline that was the essential condition for wringing out inflation and adjusting payments disequilibria. For Emminger, this was most clearly evident in the "prevailing American attitude that domestic monetary and fiscal policies should not be constrained to any significant degree by the requirements of external balance and the maintenance of a fixed dollar parity" [2]. Through liberal borrowing arrangements, the world sanctioned domestically generated inflation and fostered national irresponsibility in failing to come to grips with it. It was this tolerant environment that permitted the United States in particular to pay for its internal expansion and overseas commitments by running up payments deficits—and exporting inflation in the process.

Similarly, the German authorities argued, by acquiescing in the growing readiness to devalue, existing monetary arrangements further weakened any remaining international inhibitions on domestic expansion. Repeated depreciations, or even less conscionable forced appreciations by surplus countries, meant that inflation was incorporated into the international price structure. Indeed, some discerned a multiplier effect whereby the increased costs of imported goods in the depreciating country spurred new wage pressures to compensate for the rise in the cost of living. A more sophisticated public has freed itself from the "money illusion"—the popular belief that a dollar was a dollar (or a pound a pound) in spite of changes in its purchasing power. Moreover, there is the evident tendency, today, for the prices of industrial goods to move in tandem, regardless of cost differences. What economists call "commodity arbitrage" means that there is a natural tendency for prices internationally to shift toward a common denominator—generally the highest.

Thus a surplus country like Germany saw itself assuming the onus of sanctioning other peoples'—and world—inflation, while suffering from intermittent capital influxes (and somewhat less painful reserve accumulations) that encouraged its own inflationary pressures. The absence of any rules or understandings to prevent this international cycling of inflation was for Germany the most serious deficiency in the postwar monetary system.

This assessment of the dynamics of internationally conveyed inflation and the reciprocal interactions between inflation and currency instability was broadly accepted by all German authorities. The major variations were in the willingness to make harsh criticisms of the United States, and in judging the practical feasibility of instilling in other countries the discipline characteristic of the German economy. On both of these counts, political leader—such as Minister of Economics Helmut Schmidt and especially Chancellor Willy Brandt—were least inclined to ascribe blame to particular governments and more disposed to state the problem in terms of general systemic conditions. The preference for dispersing and neutralizing responsibility was dictated by the obvious military and political dependency on the American-led Atlantic Alliance. Germany had acknowledged this status in agreeing to a series of "offset" agreements wherein the Federal Republic committed herself to purchase military equipment from the U.S. in amounts roughly commensurate with the costs of maintaining American troops in the Federal Republic. Bonn's reliance on the U.S. for her security pervades all of German foreign policy, coloring its view of economic as well as security questions. In this instance, it did not unduly influence practical judgments (whether by elected or permanent officials) as to the American responsibility for the exchange crisis. But it did have a bearing on how the situation was represented in public statements. More important, it affected their willingness to confront Washington on a basic reordering of world economic institutions.

Applying this evaluation of the situation to the exchange crisis, German monetary authorities reached a number of conclusions that were to serve as benchmarks for their crisis behavior. One, it was futile and self-defeating to intervene on the exchange markets in a continuing attempt to maintain par values. The evidence of recent experience that central banks were unable to stem speculative flows was taken as incontrovertible. Unless major changes (harmonization of domestic monetary policy, more aggressive internal adjustment measures) were made in other facets of the system, official support operations could be of only limited effectiveness. Two, taking the mark off its peg would have immediate beneficial effects. Speculative pressures would be eased by increasing the risk of betting on an unsupported rate and, hopefully, the build-up of capital avoided. Most important, by relieving the Bundesbank of the obligation to maintain a fixed rate, monetary policy would be freed to deal with the domestic German situation. Interest rates, reserve requirements—the whole panoply of monetary instruments—need not be geared to world capital movements. They instead could be deployed as part of a restrictive policy to curb expansion and cool inflation. An upward float of the mark could also blunt American criticism of German nonchalance about racking up enormous trade surpluses.*

Three, it followed that a system of flexible or floating exchange rates had distinct attractions. Reform of the adjustment mechanism would remove the easy targets of fixed rates and stabilize capital movements. There were, to be sure, acknowledged drawbacks to be taken into account. Questions were raised about the danger of destabilizing speculation, even if less traumatic than the old speculation and spread over time, being routinized under generalized floating. Too, concern was voiced about the effects of constanting fluctuating rates on commercial transactions. Moreover, FERs (flexible exchange rates) were seen as having ambiguous implications for both global inflation and the desired freeing of government policy to address the domestic sources of performance disequilibria. The paradox of floating is that while it promises to widen the margin officials have for

*Sympathy for floating, as the basis for a new adjustment mechanism, was encouraged by the demonstrated resilience of German exports. Their competitiveness after absorbing earlier revaluations minimized worries about the adverse trade effects from the contemplated float even as Bonn acquired a talking point to use against the Americans.

internal economic management, unrestricted floating can reduce the pressures for using that freedom in a disciplined fashion since it provides a ready safety valve for a deficit (or surplus) country's currency.

In Germany, as elsewhere, judgments on these controversial issues, which were at the heart of the flourishing academic debate over floating, varied. Everyone had his own version of the truth about FERs, each estimating performance and weighing the pluses and minuses somewhat differently. The divergent interpretations being made among official actors in Germany were significant insofar as they influenced opinions on the key question of whether there should be a genuine "free float" or a "managed float." Bundesbank Chairman Karl Klassen, a commercial banker by vocation (along with most members of the bank's governing board), was most skeptical of the purer version as advocated by Dr. Emminger. The former view was shared by political leadership, including Helmut Schmidt, a reluctant floater, who saw FERs as basically an expedient. These disagreements, although not prominent at the stage of crisis management, were to surface in the debate over how to implement floating rates. (Managed floaters, on the whole, were more sensitive to the perceived dangers to German exports of a possible unlimited upvaluation of the mark and more skeptical about the stabilizing effects of market speculation. They were at once more "nationalist" than Dr. Emminger, and in disagreement on technical analyses of economic behavior as well.)

The fourth reference point for German policymakers, and on which there was total agreement, was negative view of capital controls. Theoretically the only alternative, and perhaps useful, complement to floating that could stem disruptive capital movements would be the imposition of severe restrictions on the shifting of money from one currency denomination to another, perhaps in combination with equally strict measures to "sanitize" capital inflows—i.e., preventing them from entering the money stream. The rich array of largely uncoordinated controls which had been applied intermittently by nearly all the major powers during the postwar period had been distinguished neither by their effectiveness nor their selectivity nor their integration with domestic monetary policy or the regulations of other governments. German officials held strongly the generally critical view of controls and, for special reasons of their own, were averse to their introduction. The dominant laissez-faire doctrines of the Federal Republic have as one of their tenets the superior efficiency of the market over central planning under state direction. There is a firm belief, based on both philosophical predilection and the practical achievement of the "economic miracle," that interference with the workings of the private financial markets—as through capital controls—cannot work. It is a view deeply held among senior officials in the economic ministries and largely shared (with the inevitable pragmatic qualifications in practice) by politicians of whatever partisan leaning.

The ingrained suspicion of controls was reinforced by the opposition of those offices in the Bundesbank and the Finance Ministry that would be charged with administering the system. They were unprepared to undergo the substantial staff expansion and redirection of organizational missions that the already intellectually distasteful task of minutely monitoring financial transactions would demand. It was a surprise to no one, therefore, that the Germans would spurn a French proposal for concerted controls and, while acknowledging in principle the desirability of some joint strategy for regulating the Eurocurrency markets, would commit themselves only to those actions that could be undertaken by existing bodies using established procedures—e.g., restricting the placement of reserves in Euromarket banks. The German attitude toward capital controls is a case where intellectual proclivities and policy preconceptions serve to limit a government's options. Whatever the truth about the practical efficiency of controls, it was clear that in the ideologically uncongenial atmosphere of Bonn and Frankfurt their advocacy would receive a decidedly unsympathetic hearing.

The United States

The United States was by any standard the main protagonist in the exchange drama. It held a preeminent position in the world monetary system, a status officially accorded it by the IMF's Articles of Agreement, which enthroned the dollar as the system's reserve currency, and confirmed by the dominant impact of the American economy on the world. The nub of the crisis was the contradiction between the dollar's several international roles and the exigencies of U.S. national policy. It was the chronic American payments deficit that had first begun to erode confidence in existing arrangements and had created the unstable overhang; it was the identification of liquidity growth with the dollar that gave life to the Eurocurrency market; it had been the American termination of convertibility and her unilateral devaluation that undermined its position as the system's standard of value; and it had been the Federal Reserve Bank that conceived and orchestrated the system of "swaps" for official support operations that had been the system's insurance policy against failure. Most important, active American cooperation was the sine qua non for the restoration of order and tranquility to the exchange markets. While Washington was not in a position to dictate solutions to monetary problems, it retained sufficient power to block any proposal not to its liking. The exchange crisis was a watershed in the history of postwar economic relations. It underscored the end of American hegemony; while the ensuing multilateral negotiations to control the crisis revealed just how much the system missed the American power for political construction. Resolution of the crisis was handicapped by both the lack of a catalyzing political will and the new-found American penchant for indulging neomercantile policies.

In sketching the background to the crisis, we referred cursorily to the attitudes and thinking of the Nixon Administration. It stressed the preoccupation with the adverse American trade balance, the conviction that U.S. products were discriminated against and that they needed, and properly warranted, the advantages of a drop in the par value of the dollar. While admitting that the expansionist monetary policies of the Johnson years had been a spur to global inflation, and that American deficits were destabilizing money markets, Washington rejected the idea that domestic American policy should be keyed to the task of balancing the external account. Rather the Administration approach emphasized the responsibility of surplus countries to share the burden of adjustment and continued to call for further enlargement of international borrowing facilities.

To European grumblings about the dollar's exorbitant privileges, the United States responded with complaints about the intolerable burdens on the dollar. One grievance was that "with deficits equated to sins and surpluses to virtues, moral as well as financial pressures were very much greater on deficit countries to reduce their deficits than on surplus countries to reduce surpluses" [3]. There was the accompanying grievance that the dollar's role as a reserve and intervention currency denied the U.S. the right to change its exchange rate, as did less exalted currencies in order to adjust their payments. As a result, the dollar had become progressively overvalued. The report of the Presidential Assistant for International Economic Affairs could conclude that the source of the growing crisis was "a monetary system whose inflexibility resulted in intolerable burdens being thrust on the United States" [4].

These attitudes led to a conscious decision to pursue a more nationalist tack in international economic dealings and more forcefully to assert what American officials saw as the U.S. interest. Any feelings of mercantile guilt were assuaged by the belief that since United States deficits had been incurred in good part in meeting the obligations of her military alliances, America's partners should be prepared to assist in their consolidation. John Connally had personified this aggressive American stance while Secretary of the Treasury. His "bull in the chinashop" approach, which had caused so much consternation among his diplomatic counterparts, left the office with him. But the thinking he embodied continued under his successor, George Schultz. It not only reflected the latter's own considered view of the situation, but was also the avowed policy of the White House, where President Nixon continued to take the personal interest in trade and monetary issues that dated back to his 1971 initiatives.

At the onset of the crisis the American strategy as formulated in the White House and articulated at the Treasury was two-pronged. First, a conscientious effort was made to downplay the disruptive consequences of the turbulence on the exchange markets. So long as the pressure was toward an upvaluation of other currencies, speculative forces were seen as a silent ally in the United States' campaign for a further revision of currency values. Second, it tried to avoid a narrowly focused debate on crisis measures for shoring up the dollar. Instead, Washington sought to use the discomfort of her partners to win concessions on the commercial issues that were of primary interest to the U.S.—issues that were scheduled for consideration at a trade summit instigated by the United States to be held under GATT auspices in Tokyo in September. An ancillary objective was to resist any crisis decisions that foreclosed those more fundamental reforms—i.e., reserve expansion, stronger pressures on surplus countries—that were the ulterior end of American policy.

This approach was in keeping with the strategy of "benign neglect,"* originally conceived in 1969, according to which nothing

*Sidney E. Rolfe and James L. Burtle have provided this succinct description of the benign neglect strategy:

> Do nothing. As dollars poured out of the United States, the government would not intervene to stanch the flow or to support the dollar in the foreign exchange markets. Nor would it wring its hands publicly or call for great new conferences to reform the system when Europe and Japan were resisting the key elements of reform, dollar depreciation and future flexibility, and profiting from this resistance by the additional acquisition of reserves. . . . The fate of the dollar was left in foreign hands, or to the forces of the foreign exchange markets. As dollars accumulated in foreign hands, the supply of dollars exceeded the demand. To prevent the price of dollars from devaluing, or the price of other currencies from rising vis-à-vis the dollar, the foreign central banks themselves would have to "buy" (i.e., accept) the unwanted dollars, piling up additional reserves" [5].

The origins of this "benign neglect" strategy apparently were in a Republican pre-election task force in 1968. It was associated with Professors Gottfried Haberler of Tufts and Hendrik Houthakker of Harvard, the latter a member of Nixon's Council of Economic Advisors.

would be done to relieve the burden, such as it was, on the Europeans (and Japanese) of the dollar overhang until greater sympathy was elicited for American trade and the desired dollar depreciation. "Benign neglect" was more than a tactic to improve the United States' bargaining position on monetary issues. It was indicative of a basic change in the way the United States government balanced its international obligations against national interests perceived, at times, as contrary to those obligations. The earlier postwar leadership in institution building expressed a well-developed sense of tutelary responsibility for the security and prosperity of the West. That belief included a consciously generous policy of fostering the economic strength and domestic welfare of her partners as incentives for their adherence to collective institutions. The new strategy, by contrast, was avowedly more self-centered. It set the interest of the American national economy as the benchmark of monetary and commercial policy. The distributional effects among the major participants were to be given precedence over, or at least placed on an equal footing with, the now diminished goal of Western unity.

This new approach was of a piece with the Nixon administration's vision of a decentralized, diplomatically more fluid international system and a less rigidly structured alliance network. Couched in the abstract terminology of multipolarity and shared burdens, the president and Dr. Kissinger were less concerned with any genuine devolution of power than with increasing the maneuverability of American foreign policy by reducing its formal commitments and implicit obligations. While acknowledging a genuine diminution in the power of the United States to control events all around the world or to direct the collective affairs of her allies, the administration neither favored nor expected the creation of a genuine condominium in which power and responsibility would be shared on anything like an equal basis. As Secretary Kissinger's 1973 speech ushering in The Year of Europe was to make clear, American primacy remained grounded on the fact that the U.S. was a global power, with the responsibility for the organization of a global security system, while the Europeans had only regional interests. The same held for economic affairs. As Kissinger put it, "the European Community has increasingly stressed its regional personality, the United States at the same time must act as part of, and be responsible for, a wider international trade and monetary system" [6]. The implication was that the American voice should continue to prevail in common councils even if the U.S. no longer could be counted on to make sacrifices in Europe's behalf—i.e., by accepting the financial burden of its troops in Europe or American trade deficits to make the EEC a going concern.

In a real sense, the Nixon administration sought to retain the prerogatives of American hegemony without all its specific obligations. While gaining the freedom for selective exercise of its unmatched power, the United States would enjoy the egalitarian right to play the game as "just one of the boys" when particular national interests so dictated. On economic questions, this new policy meant (1) that the United States' still substantial leverage would be openly employed, without qualms, to forestall any change on adjustment procedures or convertibility which did not accord her the freedom of revaluation; and (2) that her partners' continuing dependence on her for security would be exploited to that end.

The exchange crisis provided unmistakable evidence of this strategy. Confident that the American economy was secured against any serious damage, the American reaction was at first to do nothing. More neglect—benign or otherwise. Only when pressures against the dollar in February became severe enough to arouse concern among the central banks (the Federal Reserve included) that they were losing control over the exchanges did Washington listen to entreaties to take a hand in helping to restore orderly markets. It responded reluctantly with the second dollar devaluation—a cut averaging 6 percent against the other leading currencies. The step was taken without enthusiasm or conviction. The administration had a principled dislike for having its hand forced and would have preferred to devalue at a time of its own choosing—ideally, as part of a deal that imposed adjustment obligations on surplus countries. Accordingly, the rate changes would have looked more appealing if they had taken the form of upvaluations of her partners' currencies, with its implied shift of responsibility for adjustment.

Once the change was made, confidence was dutifully declared in the salutary and stabilizing effects that would flow from the expected assist to American exports and, thereby, to its payments account. As one Washington official explained it later, the U.S. had had "a bite of the cherry" with the rate change of December 1971 and now wanted more. Hopefully, it would be the added boost needed to make the breakthrough still awaited from the first devaluation. Undersecretary of the Treasury Paul Volcker, on a round of discussions in European capitals in February, predicted that the devaluation would lay "the basis for healthier discussion" of the situation by brightening American trade prospects and taking the wind out of the speculators' sails [7]. The reappearance a few days later of continued weakness on the exchanges was dismissed in Washington as "vicissitudes of minor importance." Meanwhile, the campaign to gain tariff concessions moved apace. Commerce Secretary Peter Peterson, at the height of the February speculation, was importuning anxious economics ministers in Europe on the trade issue in a build-up to the GATT meeting. As the crisis moved to a climax, Secretary Schultz added his voice, in a half-hearted exercise in linkage politics leaving the distinct impression that U.S. cooperation in stemming the surge of capital would be enhanced by evidence of a conciliatory attitude toward the American position on commercial questions [8].

This denigration of the exchange crisis, and its subordination to American payments preoccupations, could not be attributed exclusively to renascent mercantalism. There was a genuine belief that the fixed rate system really was not workable any longer. The Treasury felt strongly that central bank intervention had ceased to be a guarantee of rate stability. As with dominant thinking among German officials, they had come to question the viability of the commitment to fixed par values under existing volatile conditions. This analysis, again as with the German interpretation, reflected both judgments of practical feasibility and a doctrinal preference for letting the market forces operate with relative freedom. Schultz himself was a principled advocate of the free market approach, not an unusual position for a University of Chicago economics professor. While the constraints and obligations of public office, as well as his own common sense, could not permit the direct translation of theoretical belief into policy, the leaning toward market solutions and the suspicion of government regulation were real. His staff was a reinforcing factor. The Secretary brought with him into the Treasury a coterie of young economists who were tapped into the intense academic debate on fixed versus flexible exchange rates. Known in Washington as Schultz' theoreticians, they were strong champions of generalized floating and rejected the par value system altogether—a position that drew its inspiration from the monetarist private market faith. For them, floating was more than a pragmatic answer to the exchange problem; it was a vindication of their theoretical commitment.

The favorable attitude toward a flexible rate system was fed by doubts about the effectiveness of official support operations. With pressure mounting against the dollar in the first week of March, Secretary Schultz gave puhlic utterance to what had become the private American position that market forces should be "paramount" in determining rates [9]. Intellectually congenial to its formulators, seemingly dictated by circumstances, floating also nicely suited American interests. The confident expectation was that a currency float, free from central bank intervention, would see a further drop of the dollar to an equilibrium point below that reached in February. The presumed shot in the arm it would give exports could only be welcome to an administration that had invested so much political capital in its campaign to improve the terms of trade for American goods. (As an added fillip, the lowered exchange rates would act on two other elements in the overall payments equation—tourism would be discouraged; and it was supposed overseas capital investment would be similarly reduced by the diminishing buying power of the dollar in foreign markets. A turnaround on the capital account would also relieve the pressure being brought on the government by anxious Europeans to reimpose the ideologically unpalatable controls two years after they had been happily dismantled.) If things did not work out exactly as predicted under floating, the U.S. still did not have very much to lose. Retention of the dollar standard meant it could continue to deficit finance payments imbalances, while the size of the American economy made it relatively impervious to international capital movements.

The American strategy that took shape around these points did not meet with complete acceptance in Washington. It was vigorously opposed by Dr. Arthur Burns, the prestigious chairman of the Federal Reserve Board. A supporter of fixed exchange rates as the essential, secure reference point of international commerce and finance, he looked askance at the emergence of floating as a feature of monetary management (or "nonmanagement"). Holding to what was the orthodox central bank view that revaluations should be undertaken only as a last resort, when all other remedies for rectifying payments disequilbria had been tried and found wanting, he also disagreed with the second dollar devaluation in February as uncalled for. Any further American devaluations, officially declared or as the outcome of a float, would dissipate whatever little discipline remained among monetary authorities and could, he warned, trigger competitive devaluations and retaliatory capital restrictions [10].

Burns did share the belief that the primary cause of the present crisis was irresponsibly expansionist domestic monetary policies, especially in the two chronically deficit countries—the United States and the United Kingdom. They fueled inflation, swelled the money supply and therefore made impossible the adjustment of payments accounts through the correct internal measures. Faced with the now recurrent exchange crises, he complained that monetary authorities had taken altogether too leisurely and complaisant an attitude in resorting to devaluations and partial floats that were de facto revaluatopms [11]. The answer then to the present disorder was closer cooperation among the central banks in controlling the money supply and interest rates, the pursuit of contractionary domestic policies where indicated, continued official intervention on the exchange markets and perhaps the selective introduction of controls on capital movements—all part of a sober effort to restore confidence in monetary stability and the capabilities of monetary authorities.

This striking divergence of opinion between, on the one hand, Secretary Schultz and the bulk of the Treasury officialdom which supported their chief's position with minor differences of emphasis and, on the other, Chairman Burns, who received equivalent backing from the Fed's Board of Governors and senior staff, on first glance seemed all the more surprising for the core of economic beliefs they held in common. Both were monetary and fiscal conservatives who in principle stressed the virtues of restraint in government spending and felt little compunction about the dampening of expansionist tendencies when the economy was thought to be overheating. Both men were monetarists who accorded a prominent place to money supply and the terms of its availability in explaining economic phenomena. Both were defenders of the free market, inclined toward state reserve in exercising its powers of economic control and direction. Both were generally internationalist in their recognition that American prosperity depends to some immeasurable degree on world conditions and acknowledging the United States' obligation to maintain a stable structure of cooperation. Yet they came to diametrically different conclusions on the question of floating exchange rates.

The answer seems to lie in the different responsibilities attendant upon their official positions, the experiences and obligations associated with them, and the attitudes to which they give rise. As we noted earlier, there are features of central banking that distinguish its practitioners from officials in other economic departments of government. They have specific undertakings to perform, exchange intervention high among them; they have fraternal relations with their counterparts; and they do have that measure of political independence. It is not unexpected therefore that central bankers should be hesitant about phasing out the official support operations which had been their meat and drink. Or that in the course of conducting them they should acquire a considerable confidence in the ability of "practical and well-informed men" to agree on the proper equilibrium points for currencies. Or any less surprising that members of the Fed's board should resist being placed in the position of appearing before their central bank colleagues at a monthly BIS (Bank for International Settlements) meeting in Basle to explain why the U.S. government was prepared to engage in monetary brinksmanship, and to tempt the fates of the exchange markets, in order to increase American leverage on trade issues, (as was the case for Governor Dewey Daane who attended the BIS sessions in his capacity as chairman of the Fed's Open Market Committee); and should be especially sensitive about the mercantile tone of American policy. And even less reason to be surprised that Mr. Charles Coombs, who was the architect of the swap arrangements (and special manager for foreign currency operations), should feel most strongly on this score.

By comparison, Treasury officials not only shared these experiences in much diluted form (their involvement in these forums being less intense, their international responsibilities less concrete), but also by virtue of their position were more responsive to American economic conditions and more atuned to political pressures. These pressures came from within and from outside the administration. Proximity to political power implies at once paramount authority and susceptibility to group and partisan conflicts, actual or anticipated. An administration edgy about unrest on the home front was sensitive to these considerations. The intensifying trade union campaign for surcease from the exportation of jobs; growing protectionist sentiment in the Congress (given shape in the Burke-Hartke Bill); the new aggressiveness of those domestically based manufacturing interests hurt by foreign competition (a group well represented inside the Administration by now Commerce Secretary Peter Peterson)—these were a not insignificant combination of forces pushing for a more nationalist position on trade toward which the White House was already inclined for its own reasons. It demanded a Treasury Secretary whose thinking was in line with the thrust of its policy. Schultz was more than just sympathetic. Intellectually compatible with the measures that policy indicated, and free from any professional attachment to the existing adjustment mechanism, he was a dedicated supporter of FERs. (His principal deputy, Undersecretary Volcker, had been more of a skeptic. Over the years the latter had made a personal odyssey, along with many others, from an outright rejection of floating rates as an idea spawned in the universities and best left there, to a realistic acceptance of their inevitability. By the winter of 1973, he had come to support FERs as a substitute for the manifestly impractical par value system. But his conversion was never total. He still retained doubts about many of the virtues other, more convinced, advocates saw in floating and continued to see a role for government intervention under certain conditions.)

Two features of the Schultz-Burns disagreement are especially noteworthy in the context of this analysis. First, the differences in priority and emphasis that led the Treasury to support a more "nationalistic approach" had an affinity with both organizational roles and the intellectual predilections of the individual concerned.

(It perhaps would have been a more interesting case for analysis if organizational role and personal proclivity had pulled in opposite directions.) The speculative judgments one made of how floating would work dovetailed with interpretations that were being made about the nature of the crisis. The preferred prescription found the right diagnosis. It was convenient that a Treasury Secretary obedient to White House directives aimed at acquiring preferential advantages for the U.S. should be philosophically inclined toward that solution, of a system problem, which advanced that end. It was no less logical that Chairman Burns, with greater distance from the White House and practiced in the ways of the old system, should prefer an alternative that placed greater stock in central bank intervention.*

Second, the Federal Reserve was disposed to include a larger slice of the latitudinal dimension of the problem in its approach, at least insofar as it expressed greater concern about the international economic repercussions of the avowed American policy. The Treasury and official American position can be said to have encompassed more of the social dimension in terms of (1) its sensitivity to the domestic context of policy, and (2) the Administration's wider foreign policy objectives. Paradoxically, in this instance, the former's broader, systemic definition of the problem pointed to a more narrowly focused answer since the Fed's skeptical view of flexible exchange rates meant a reversion to conventional forms of cooperation. However, if FERs are interpreted as a form of monetary laissez faire on an international scale, then their innovation would weaken the strain toward synchronization of national policies and collective oversight of the currency markets.

Whatever might be the real results of one approach or another, it is striking that preferences were keyed to short term considerations. For FER supporters in government these were the benefits accruing to the American payments account; for its Federal Reserve opponents, the supreme importance of maintaining stable par values through central bank management. Neither outlook was distinguished by its reach in searching for comprehensive remedies that could restructure monetary institutions for the long haul.

France

Among the major actors in the exchange crisis, France was least sympathetic to the American position and most willing to criticize it

*Actually, Burns had some discretion in choosing just how "distant" he wanted to be. At times, he was fully prepared to assist the Republican President on the political front. In late 1971 and 1972 he swallowed his monetary conservatism long enough to bail out an endangered Administration by turning on the money spigot. Economic orthodoxy is a sometime thing.

publicly. Confrontation in the monetary arena had been a characteristic of strained Franco-American relations over the structure of the Atlantic Alliance for more than a decade [12]. General de Gaulle, in his unstinting efforts to diminish what he saw as the United States" hegemonial domination of her European allies, had sought to exploit the dollar's vulnerability by attacking its reserve status—e.g., demanding payment in gold for the dollar obligations it held.

De Gaulle's plan to dethrone the dollar was an integral part of his strategy for cutting the Americans down to diplomatically manageable size. As Robert Gilpin has explained, discontinuing the privileged position of the dollar meant "[t]he United States would have to expend real wealth in order to maintain and/or expand its hegemony. If other nations refused to accept any more dollars and demanded gold, the United States would be forced to bring its payments into balance and to liquidate [or at least retrench] its global economic and military position" [13]. French efforts to unite the Europeans in a campaign of resistance against economic domination by the dollar concentrated not on the grand political vision, but instead, sought to arouse latent sensitivities about the invasion of American investment capital with its implied threat to national powers of economic management and resource allocation. As with other facets of his grand strategy, de Gaulle could will the ends much more easily than he could the means. The political goals of his monetary battles with Washington frightened potential European sympathizers desirous of a strong American military and political presence on the continent. Moreover, they also saw little virtue in the General's one substantive proposal—a return to the gold standard. It properly was deemed unworkable and a return to the rigid system discredited in the world economic collapse of the 1930s.

De Gaulle's successors lacked both his passion for combat and his confidence in France's ability to engage in it successfully. While muting the chorus of political criticism which was background to the General's economic maneuvering, President Pompidou and Finance Minister Valéry Giscard d'Estaing nonetheless shared many of his attitudes about the United States' abuse of the dollar's unique status. They too were unhappy about its privileged position which enabled the U.S. to liability finance the enormous deficits that were chalked up in good part due to the activities of American-based multinationals buying up a growing share of European industry and to cover the costs of a global foreign policy some of whose manifestations were seen as antithetical to French interests. And they too spoke of an equality of rights and privileges.

Washington's termination of dollar convertibility, and the initial dollar devaluation, heightened the dilemma for the French whose succinct critique of the situation was matched by the absence of a persuasive prescription. For they were unclear as to just how the dollar overhang might be consolidated and dissolved, uncertain as to the form an alternative reserve currency might take and how it might be installed without disrupting the international economy. The lack of solutions did not abate anxiety though. France was most concerned about the threat to her exports posed by a cheap dollar. Latent doubts about the competitiveness of French industry, and nervousness about the fragility of present prosperity, lie just below a confident surface. They are accentuated by fears of the social unrest that would follow from any marked rise in unemployment as would result from a downturn in exports. Abiding concern about unemployment serves as the most prominent reference point for France's economic planners, just as inflation does for the Federal Republic. It was to protect her trade position that France had introduced the two tier rate system in 1971 in the hope of partially insulating commerce from the impact of capital movements on the exchange rate. So it was in keeping with the tenets of French policy that at the height of the March crisis it should be made known that "the sole concern that motivates the chief of state is . . . to consolidate at all costs the breakthrough by French exports and to do nothing which on the contrary favors imports to the detriment of the national product" [14].

The strong downward pressures on the dollar and the growing sentiment to relieve the central banks of their commitment to pegged rates were extremely disquieting to Paris. Disorder was distressing not only because it threatened to remove control over the nation's economic fate from the hands of national authorities—a prospect worrisome enough for the rational positivists that pervade French officialdom—but also because the crisis was seen as creating conditions conducive to American policy objectives. Accordingly, the Ministry of Finance and the Banque de France were both adamant that the U.S. not be allowed to exploit the situation to win a further devaluation of the dollar. For the advantageous terms of trade it would gain could only harm French export interests while enhancing the United States' ability to cover its questionable external expenditures. In this way, a strong intellectual preference for government regulation of economic forces converged with obvious national interests to reinforce a policy opposed to greater rate flexibility.

Ideological predilections (as elsewhere) did not produce clear formulas for resolving the dilemmas of the world's monetary system. They were expressed in general attitudes skeptical of any doctrinally uncongenial plan (floating rates) and an attraction to those ideas that suited national interests and thinking alike (capital controls). The very lack of an encompassing reform program focused attention selectively on that aspect of the problem—a threatening devaluation for France's commercial competitors—most pertinent to the French economy. Policy was more clearly aimed at preventing these adverse developments than it sought distinctly favorable, innovative solutions.

Speaking on February 21, immediately after the second dollar devaluation, Giscard noted disapprovingly that "For a year and a half everything has been done to move in the direction of the disorganization of the monetary system, since we have had successively the floating of the major currencies, and [their] inconvertibility." To increase flexibility "in a sense would consecrate the present disorder and acquiesce in the disappearance of any security . . . for anyone" [15]. Rather, the imperative need was for the immediate restoration of exchange order that then would permit a general reconstruction of the system. For the moment, the priority should be a recommitment to central bank intervention in "a concerted defense against speculation." This also meant the imposition of strict exchange and capital controls. On this issue, the French clearly stood out from their partners. They were unique both in the equanimity with which they viewed draconian controls and in their belief that they could be made to work successfully without stultifying productive movements.

The reasons for this faith are no mystery. France has a long tradition of administrative activism and economic planning. French authorities exercise a far tighter control over the country's banking system than do other Western nations (indeed the three largest banks are government-owned); there is a deep-seated belief in the virtues and efficacy of state action; and their extraordinarily able corps of *haut fonctionnaires* has the powers to match their technocratic impulses. As a practical matter, a regime of floating exchange rates threatened to upset the calculations that are the basis for the French government's brand of indicative planning. Instinctively, the French government's reaction to an economic challenge is government intervention, coupled to a low threshold of tolerance for the unpredictable free market—whether operating nationally or internationally. Equally in keeping with French tradition, the call for capital controls was predicated on voluntary cooperation by national government authorities and no proposal was offered for making obligatory commitments to the rules whose implementation would be overseen, if not administered, by an international consortium. The French preoccupation was protecting national interests and national powers of decision both.

These attitudes prevailed throughout the economic ministries, and dominated the thinking of the President and his *conseil.* In France there was probably less difference of opinion on the exchange rate issue than in any other leading country. The Director of the Banque de France, Olivier Wormser, held views nearly identical to those which had been expressed by M. Pompidou and M. Giscard. He was himself often quoted in a similar vein. On only two points of emphasis was there a noticeable divergence. Wormser, in his public remarks, placed more stress on inflation, both as a cause of the present crisis and as one of its most pernicious effects. (The preoccupation with inflation, as this review suggests, is a hallmark of central bank thinking in all countries.) Echoing the analyses and critiques made by the Bundesbank and the Federal Reserve, he pressed for an end to overly expansionist domestic policies and a contraction of credit [16]. France was not excluded from his strictures. Like his central bank colleagues elsewhere, Wormser clearly was less sensitive to the popular demands for increases in welfare and more tolerant of a downturn in economic activity. Monetary officials, by vocation, place greater weight on the stability of the currency, and on financial security, than they do on expansion for its own sake. Their performance scorecard is graded according to their success in maintaining the purchasing power of money. Economics Ministers, and particularly, in France, the Planning Commission, are judged by the broader criteria of growth. The relative independence of central banks affords them the freedom to proclaim their monetary conservatism, even if rarely the opportunity for acting on it. Certainly, in France, their margin for independent action is narrowly circumscribed.

The French formulation of the problem, therefore, was temporally rather restricted in that it asked primarily as to France's short term interests and the immediate threats posed to them. The French government was ambivalent about an encompassing approach. Intellectually, they definitely linked the exchange crisis to their wider assessment of the dollar-dependent monetary system's inherent deficiencies, and beyond it to their continuing vision of a multipolar world system. Paris' position differed from that of her European partners, and was a mirror image of the American attitude in associating economic relations with the overall Atlantic relationship. The attempt to bind her EEC associates in a united front against the Americans was to follow in the recent tradition of frustrated plans, foundering on the opposition of her partners to any important revision of the political compact with the U.S., as well as differences in the calculation of economic interest.

In the prevailing climate of European official opinion unfavorable to a reconstruction of monetary institutions à la francaise, the optimal strategy was a more modest one. One, it refrained from pushing for a simultaneous discussion of monetary issues with other alliance questions; second, it concentrated on protecting France's commercial stake as the crisis deliberations went their unpredictable way. To achieve her goals, there were tactical linkages which Paris was prepared, indeed desirous, to make. Specifically, the French moved to make the connection between any idea of floating rates and the trade negotiations that were moving on a parallel track toward an autumn GATT meeting. Any further revaluation of the dollar was threatening to breach the defenses being built against the mounting American campaign for commercial concessions from her trading partners. France was keen that the United States not be permitted to achieve cost free, under the guise of crisis measures, what she otherwise would have to extract in protracted GATT deliberations.

The United Kingdom

It is indicative of Britain's economic decline that she should appear well along in any discussion of national positions. Under the Bretton Woods system, the pound stood alongside the dollar as a reserve currency where it could serve to consolidate the monetary affairs of the extensive sterling bloc of countries. As in the larger sphere of world politics, Britain saw her monetary role as supportive of the U.S. in reordering the world system shattered by WW II. Her special status was acknowledged in the weight of Britain's voice in the IMF Secretariat and in the prominence her official representatives had in international forums.

That position, and influence, was to decline as the weakness of the British economy and the severity of her payments problems were to become apparent. Sterling was the crisis currency of the early and mid-1960s, as the dollar was to be at the end of the decade. Deterioration of her payments situation, reflecting (among other things) the country's unfavorable resource balance and the structural defects of her industry, placed British governments in a now familiar dilemma. Sterling being a reserve currency, there was a keen desire (especially in the Bank of England and the Treasury) to avoid a devaluation which, by undermining confidence in the pound, would undercut the UK's prestige and financial place in the world. (An immediate, practical concern was that devaluation would constrict sterling's use as a transaction currency and cut the invisible earnings from London's functioning as a great financial center.) While the argument often was made more with regard to national amour-propre than in strictly economic terms, the status factor could not fail to leave its mark on governments still struggling to redefine a more modest world role for the UK while trying to get a handle on chronic internal problems. Labor governments were especially susceptible to these arguments in support of maintaining the fixed rate of sterling. Devaluation, then, was something to be avoided. Yet internal adjustments through austerity programs were also ruled out by the overriding national commitment to full employment—a commitment that was sealed in the tacit compact of postwar party politics [17]. The only out was borrowing, and that too had its limits.

Despite substantial international rescue efforts—through the IMF, General Agreement to Borrow (which expanded borrowing facilities in the early 1960s with the specific purpose of saving the pound) and joint central bank interventions—sterling was fated to be devalued and gradually to cede its place as a reserve currency. The bullet was bitten in 1967 when Harold Wilson's government finally chose to abandon the fight for parity in order to salvage its domestic program. Political discretion is the better part of monetary valor. The first devaluation, and subsequent ones, though, did not succeed in turning around Britain's trade account. What had by the late 1960s become the perpetual sterling crisis was overtaken, and partially subsumed, within the growing dollar crisis. Their interests, as chronic deficit countries, were in some important respects parallel.

For one thing, as a deficit country with pronounced borrowing needs, the UK shared the American concern for new liquidity creation, the raising of borrowing limits and the latter's benevolent view of deficit financing. Second, their earlier, unsuccessful—and expensive—goal-line defenses of sterling left British monetary authorities with a favorable opinion of greater exchange rate flexibility. In June 1972, following the German and Japanese examples, the UK took sterling off its peg and let it float. In their case, it was intended to relieve pressures on the downside. The step was taken in the correct expectation that the pound would fall once left to its own devices and produce the desired, if less predictable, effect of spurring exports. When the exchange crisis erupted the next March in the frenzied flight from the dollar, sterling found itself an innocent victim, experiencing an unanticipated, unwanted and unwarranted rise. There was much to be uneasy about.

Exchange disorder was itself unwelcome. It was all the more irksome when one of its side effects was to contradict British commercial interests by upvaluing a currency, vis-à-vis the dollar, that by all rights had no business being appreciated. The immediate British goal, therefore, was to end this unnatural development by restoring stability to the money markets, so that monetary authorities could take a firm hand on things. Reestablishing a modicum of control was essential in order to restrain the indiscriminate downward float of the dollar that forced Britain to share the costs of an improved American trade balance. London's second objective, looking just beyond the immediate problem, was an agreement on a more flexible adjustment mechanism that would permit routine rate changes in an orderly fashion—i.e., that allowed controlled devaluations after proper notification of one's trading partners and according to general guidelines and which would avoid both pressures for internal adjustments and/or an excessive strain on borrowing facilities.

This was the assessment being made, with slight variation, at the Bank of England and in the Treasury alike. The differences were in the relative emphasis placed on the apparently divergent goals of expansion and containing inflation. As in France and just about everywhere else, monetary officials at the Bank of England, whose paramount concern is sound money, placed greatest stress on the latter. The Treasury, which had tended to share this conservative attitude, had been partially persuaded by the increasingly popular view that a period of sustained growth could produce the industrial renovation that would break the British economy free of its payments-induced stop-go cycle. Although the short term inflationary costs remained a source of anxiety, the Treasury was placed somewhere between the expansion-minded cabinet and the critical Bank of England view of this strategy.

Both departments would have no truck with capital controls of the sort advocated by France. The UK had introduced her own comparatively stringent exchange controls a few years earlier as part of a plan to right her balance of payments. While reasonably effective in restricting the outflow of corporate investment capital, and on tourism, they met with less success in grounding private funds. To the inherent difficulties of monitoring the intricate movements of money were added two other factors. One, British government authorities are traditionally reluctant to encroach on private commercial and financial domains. The prevailing political culture does accord state authority substantial powers of decisional autonomy and there is a strong tradition of deference to national leadership. But it is coupled with strictures about the impropriety of infringing upon the private preserves of economic associations. By comparison with the French, certainly, the British lack a doctrine of technocratic positivism, its faith in state intervention and the elaborate administrative apparatus for implementing detailed controls. Second, rigid controls threatened to interfere with the City's role as a financial center dependent on the free flow of funds from account to account, currency to currency—a role that has been deemed a considerable national asset.

Japan

Although the world's third industrial power, a leading trading nation and possessing one of the sounder currencies, Japan played a largely passive role in the numerous meetings and conferences that proliferated before, during and after the crisis. This unassertiveness was very much in keeping with the withdrawn, reticent position she had assumed generally in world politics since WW II. On issues affecting the framework of the international economic system, Japan at once benefited from the network of cooperative institutions that flourished under American tutelage and drew special advantage from the protectionist policies allowed her by an indulgent protector. Export subsidies and the assiduous cultivation of markets, high import tariffs and severe restrictions on capital investments from abroad (although not technology) all had helped build Japan's remarkable postwar prosperity while assuring healthy payments surpluses. They also gave the country partial insulation from the financial crises that perturbed the Western economies. In a sense, she had had the best of commercial interdependence and suffered least from monetary and financial interdependence.

The imposed modesty of Japan's postwar policies fitted her tradition of historical isolation and her more modern practice of selfsufficient enterprise. Both past experience and contemporary circumstance encouraged a mercantalism that took for granted the nonzero-sum part of the international economy, while an ingrained sense of vulnerability made her cautious about either assuming an active leadership role or relinquishing the advantages accorded her as an economic and political dependent. Japan though was not simply a bystander. Her bilateral trade dispute with the United States that came to a head in August 1971 had a real, if largely indirect, impact on trans-Atlantic relations. The special trade privileges in which Washington saw itself acquiescing to facilitate Japanese reconstruction and political stability had by the late 1960s become a bone of contention to an administration exercised by the steady erosion of the American trade position and mildly paranoid about her partners' barriers to American exports. The United States' deficit with Japan equaled nearly 80 percent of the total trade imbalance. Japanese reluctance to dismantle trade obstacles stopped being a nuisance and began to look more ominous. The drastic "Nixon shock" of 1971, including the imposition of import levies, was motivated by anger over Tokyo's dilatoriness in giving concrete expression to vague promises of reform made by Prime Minister Sato a year earlier. The Europeans, with some justification, saw themselves as suffering from Washington's pique over the Japanese actions—or lack of action—that led to retaliation across the board. The American retort was that the barriers to Japanese imports erected by the Europeans channeled her exports into the US.

During the interregnum between the Nixon shock and the 1973 exchange crisis, the Japanese—as we noted earlier—sought to avoid further revaluation of the yen through the expediency of a "dirty float." Easing exchange pressures by absolving themselves of the commitment to a fixed rate, Japanese monetary authorities made generous use of widely employed subterfuges to contain the actual movements. When the dollar caved in, in February, threatening a more extensive change in the yen's exchange rate, their immediate worry was to stave off any further upvaluation of their currency. With this objective uppermost in mind, Tokyo opposed a generalized free float and instead urged a system of managed floating to be directed by the central banks and to be coupled with selective capital controls. Like the French, Japanese officials were anxious that the United States might use the crisis to adjust the terms of trade to American advantage. Hence, they were deeply skeptical about an unrestricted float and determined to resist any American plan that withheld cooperation pending her partners' making trade concessions. Unlike the French, the Japanese were inhibited by near total dependence on the American security umbrella. She was deferential toward American leadership and harbored no alternative vision of a drastic rearrangement of global power.

SUMMARY

What does this review of national governments' perceptions of the exchange crisis say about their approach to questions of collective economic management? Three features stand out:

First, there is a marked tendency for political leadership and organizational actors to break down the problem into its several component parts. They focus on those themes, and concern themselves with those effects, that touch their own interest most directly. Foremost among those interests, of course, is national economic well-being. But they also include: a government's effective power to influence the framework of collective action; in the wider sphere of security needs, the preservation of cordial relations with a protective ally (*or* the assertion one's independence from an overbearing ally); and for agency officials, an undiminished and, hopefully, amplified voice in the councils of economic decision, whatever new monetary arrangements come into play. Sustaining these perceptions of interest, and having a natural affinity for them, are doctrines, philosophies and analytical models. Ideas, too, are interests in which actors have a stake, to which they become committed and which color the way they understand and interpret reality.

Second, the tendency to disaggregate issues intellectually means that remedial measures are directed selectively at those facets of the problem which are of greatest personal—i.e., national—interest. Frankfurt monetary officials, gravely worried about the disruptive influx of capital, concentrated on means to rescue domestic monetary policy by sparing the deutschemark the unwelcome attentions of currency speculators. The United States, comfortably insulated from the worst of exchange market turbulence, saw in the crisis occasion to press its new strategy calling for burden-sharing and commercial concessions from her allies that could firm up the dollar-dependent monetary system it dominated. For France, the name of the game was defense of export industries. If the crisis could be used to advance her political goal of trimming American influence, fine. But the main thing was to block any move that would license Washington to devalue the dollar as a substitute for more basic reform of her profligate ways. Britain's anxieties, diverse and all well-founded, made her both hesitant to repledge adherence to the old rules and charry of proposals entailing new obligations. Self-interest in her case dictated an ultrapragmatism that skeptically scanned any new item on the agenda to detect whatever complications it might present for her harried economic policymakers.

National preferences therefore were very much a function of economic circumstance. The dilemmas of collective economic management in a partially integrated system are common to all its members, but each must grapple with particular manifestations of it. A nation's personal situation provides the angle of vision from which to judge the relative worth—and effectiveness—of measures to achieve even a mutually acknowledged goal. The resulting disagreements take multiple forms—conflicts over distributional effects, differences of opinion as to what cause-and-effect theory best represents the reality they confront, or divergent estimates of official capabilities. Values and interests converge and reinforce each other. Doctrines and theories, though, do cross national boundaries, influencing and being influenced by national economic conditions and political circumstance. They structure and sustain perceptions of what the economic stakes are and how they might be protected.

NOTES TO CHAPTER 2

1. Paper presented at the tenth lecture meeting of the Per Jacobsson Foundation in Basle, Switzerland, June 16, 1973. Reprinted in *How Well Are Fluctuating Exchange Rates Working?* Hearings before the Subcommittee on International Economics of the Joint Economic Committee, Congress of the United States (Washington, D.C.: U.S. Government Printing Office, 1973), p. 201.

2. Ibid., p. 206.

3. Address of Arthur F. Burns delivered May 12, 1972 in Montreal, reprinted in *The Smithsonian Agreement.*

4. *Economic Report of the President 1972* (Washington, D.C.: U.S. Government Printing Office).

5. Sidney E. Rolfe and James I. Burtle, *The Great Wheel: The World Monetary System* (New York: Quadrangle, 1973), p. 99.

6. Henry Kissinger "The Year of Europe." Address to the Associated Press Editors, New York City, April 23, 1973.

7. *Le Monde,* February 18, 1973.

8. *Financial Times,* March 5, 1973.

9. Ibid.

10. *The Times* of London, February 21, 1973.

11. *The Times* of London, March 8, 1973.

12. Franco-American conflicts in the economic sphere are given detailed treatment by David F. Calleo and Benjamin M. Rowland *America and the World Political Economy* (Bloomington: Indiana University Press, 1973).

13. *Le Monde,* March 14, 1973.

14. *Le Monde,* February 21, 1973.

15. *Le Monde,* March 16, 1973.

16. *Le Monde,* April 23, 1973.

17. See the analysis of the British dilemma by Susan Strange *Sterling and British Policy* (London: Oxford University Press, 1971).

Chapter 3

Negotiation

The diversity of outlooks and interests that the participants brought to the multilateral diplomacy of fashioning a response to the exchange crisis could not obscure a common stake in putting an end to disruption on the currency markets. As the least common denominator of universal concern, it encouraged a tacit agreement to simplify the discussions by narrowing the definition of the problem. Differences, it was hoped, could be made more tractable by finessing those contentious issues of monetary reform—reserve standards, liquidity creation, convertibility—which were some degrees removed from the immediate crisis. Hence the understanding that the matter at hand should be expanded only so far as was necessary to assure a stable adjustment procedure and to restore a modicum of order to the exchanges.

Although there was no illusion that this represented anything other than an arbitrary delimitation of the problem, the urgency of the situation was seen pragmatically as excluding what surely would be a frustrating attempt at general renovation. (France was the odd man out. Her repeated efforts to make the connection, by some means or other, between the crisis talks and the trade and convertibility questions met with little favor and were to elicit only reiterated pledges of later consideration.) Each participant did see the situation as both opening opportunities to achieve more far-reaching monetary objectives and posing equally real dangers of the system's being reordered according to someone else's design. Lacking confidence that they could make the process work to their advantage—and not entirely sure that they could predict outcomes of any major innovation—most governments would rest content with a surcease from the tribulations of the moment.

THE MARCH EMERGENCY

By general agreement the emergency meetings of officials in March 1973 were restricted to a search for means of protection against excessive capital flows. For all intents and purposes only two alternatives presented themselves—exchange controls, or taking currencies off their pegs and letting them float. The design and concerted implementation of controls faced insuperable difficulties. First, since everyone agreed that there are important, constructive purposes served by international capital movements (furthering system efficiency by responding to differential costs and prices, encouraging entrepreneurship and so forth), there was the dilemma of differentiating between legitimate, long term investment and short term interest-sensitive and exchange-rate-sensitive movements. Second, the structure of capital markets varies markedly from country to country. Information about them often is either incomplete or organized differently by the collating agencies and the administrative means might be lacking for acquiring and using it. Third, in some countries—e.g., Germany, and to a lesser extent the UK and the United States—there are philosophical or traditional reasons for opposing the type of encroachment on private financial activity that controls imply. These attitudes are reinforced in some instances by monetary authorities' well-defined conception of their role, which in this area is a self-limiting one. Fourth, for controls to be effective they must be applied conscientiously by all parties according to an explicit set of rules. No such assumption of unanimity could reasonably be made. Nor, after the experience of the 1971–1972 dirty floats, was there abundant faith in the trustworthiness of other governments. The unavoidable conclusion was that capital would not be quarantined or its movement channeled.

With the option of exchange controls discarded, everything pointed to the inauguration of a floating rate system. If fixed rates could not be defended against speculative forces, if there were no reasonable way to contain capital shifts, then the only alternative to a perilous train of forced revaluations—and possible collapse of the money markets—was to let rates fluctuate as determined by market pressures. This situationally overwhelming logic, inescapable though it was, could not simply be reified as an international accord. For one thing, floating had long been a heretical idea. It ran against the grain of monetary officials, and governments generally, who believed strongly in the importance of an unchanging standard of value against which to gauge economic transactions. The life of an economic manager is arduous enough without the added burden of not knowing just how much one's money is worth.

Floating, as theory, had rapidly won favor in the academic community, whose members were by no means reticent in offering their advice that stubborn adherence to the par value system guaranteed perpetual, and eventually crippling, exchange crises. Considerable sympathy for this view gradually had been elicited in some economics ministries, and fewer central banks. But belief in generalized floating was still very much a minority view, suspect in most eyes. What gave it new credibility and appeal was the mounting crisis in which all the other possible answers were shown wanting.

Both sympathizers and skeptics of flexible exchange rates admitted that a switchover to floating was not simple or painless. A number of significant adjustments would have to be made and important conditions met. At the heart of the problem were the three primary international currencies—the dollar, the deutschemark and sterling. Some understanding had to be reached as to their role in the conjectured new scheme of things. In effect that meant restating the monetary relationship among the major currency zones. Germany and the UK were primary actors in the international dialogue, and also critical to any arrangement of the monetary affairs of the European Community and its economic satellites. The former was its leading economic force. The latter was uncomfortably perched between its residual sterling bloc commitments and its still embryonic EEC ties.

The foremost condition for launching the generalized float was an accord among members of the EEC on the coordinated monetary planning that would protect Community institutions against the potentially disruptive effects of fluctuations among member currencies. Some of the most critical and controversial elements of the EEC's integrated policies were predicated on careful calculations of shared costs that presumed their fixed values. Revaluations within the Community of course had occurred previously. Those changes had been willful acts of governments on which there was prior consultation and opportunity was provided to make the necessary adjustments. The prospect of continually shifting rates would greatly complicate the task of refining programs and stipulating budgets. Moreover, outstanding among the proclaimed goals for further integration announced in October 1972—at the time of Britain's accession to membership—was progress toward monetary union. The impending introduction of FERs jeopardized that objective unless an outline for monetary unification could be agreed upon in a much foreshortened time span. More positively, in the eyes of Community activists, the crisis created the unexpected opportunity for a breakthrough in Community construction by greatly strengthening the case for a thoroughgoing harmonization of national policies. (As an additional benefit, a joint monetary program might diffuse the effects of capital flows, thereby blunting their impact.)

The weeks of late February and early March saw the elaborate machinery of Community diplomacy unlimber itself. Bilateral and collective discussions at several levels of government overlapped and intersected—all accompanied by a continuing dialogue with Washington. There emerged from this process a coalition of convenience among those diverse individuals and governments who, perceiving some positive advantage in FERs, encouraged the idea of a joint European float against the dollar. The coalition included (1) officials who believed that the paramount goal of restoring exchange stability could only be attained by giving more play to currency changes even while affirming the responsibility of government authorities for maintaining orderly conditions; (2) pro-Marketeers who sought to advance the cause of regional integration through monetary union; and (3) the United States, which looked favorably on a Community float as a step that would facilitate the task of agreeing on the terms of a more flexible adjustment mechanism for the world monetary system as a whole.

American support came early in the crisis. Undersecretary Volcker, during his European tour to explain the second dollar devaluation, used the occasion to call for the linking of the major European currencies in a joint float and privately expressed American backing of such a move. There was a touch of irony to the American position. Over the preceding years of growing monetary and commercial conflict, the United States' ardent support for European integration had cooled noticeably. She clearly was disinclined to encourage an economic rival for the sake of the greater political solidarity of the West. Yet a positive view of monetary union was dictated by Washington's own interest in smoothing the path for the introduction of floating. There also was the practical consideration that the European float would be dominated by the deutschemark whose strength would pull up other Community currencies with it.

The theme of a Community float soon was being voiced independently by prominent Europeans. A week later, Guido Carli, the director of the Bank of Italy and his country's most powerful economic policymaker, argued the case for a float and urged steps toward its organization [1]. It was a view in keeping with the Italian central banks' preference for the flexibility that would permit managed floating of the unstable lira; its desire to win assurances of support from the German mark in any defense of the lira that might be required; and its wish to use the commitment to a Community position to buttress Carli's campaign within the Italian government for the more stringent monetary and fiscal policies that he saw as essential for stabilizing an overheated economy. He was backed by EEC High Commissioner François-Xavier Ortoli who, in an interview with *La Stampa*, [2] also proposed "a concerted float of European currencies vis-à-vis the dollar." Ortoli's attitude was a nice blend of the commission interest in pushing the cause of Community construction with the French policy of forging a unified European policy to confront the US as an equal on monetary questions.

Germany, for the reasons we discussed, was a strong advocate of floating, and Finance Ministry officials made it clear that, unless a common approach was agreed upon, they would take unilateral action—releasing the mark and letting it float on its own. However, on the specific question of a Community float, German officials had mixed feelings. The institutional health of the Community obviously could benefit from the impetus toward integration and harmonization that floating would generate (European integration being a somewhat tarnished, but still powerful idea). The second attraction was that the expected upward float of the mark—which, if the conventional economic wisdom had any validity, at some point had to begin having an adverse effect on her trade balances—would be moderated by tying it to the relatively weak currencies of her partners. On the other hand, as a matter of short term interest, an upvaluation of the mark, unrestrained by the obligations of joint float, would lighten the Bonn government's payments to the increasingly unpopular agricultural fund to which Germany was the main contributor and France the main beneficiary. More significantly, if the British and the Italians were to participate in the float, the Bundesbank would be obliged to commit German reserves in support of the inherently weak pound and lira, a prospect that was viewed with consternation among economic officials (including Finance Minister Schmidt) and was actively opposed by the Bundesbank.

The issue was decided by the firm intervention of Chancellor Brandt who launched a diplomatic campaign to promote the joint float as the cornerstone of monetary union. It was a classic case of higher political authority imposing itself on ministerial officials (and, in this case, on cabinet colleagues), taking an initiative to achieve what was deemed an overriding end of state. Brandt believed, in his words, that "a joint approach to international monetary questions [is] a crucial test of the Common Market's ability to work together"

[3]. Community development was a political objective of the utmost importance in the chancellor's view of Germany's—and Europe's—future. The steps which must be taken to achieve it might run counter to calculations of immediate economic interest, and the cautious councils of officialdom, they should be pursued nonetheless. (In the terminology used earlier, Brandt had extended his definition of the problem along the temporal axis, and broadened it to introduce and give special weight to the requirements he saw for the long term political stability that could only be realized in political union. It was a form of political linkage inspired by the vision of a future international milieu rather than a perception of a purely national interest. Appeals to that goal were made on behalf of a preferred formula for dealing with the practical matter at hand.)

Brandt's efforts concentrated on the British, whose participation in the joint float (or "snake" as it became known) he thought essential to make the project work as a catalyst for Community integration. It also would serve to speed up the pace of Britain's assimilation into the EEC. In talks with Prime Minister Edward Heath in Bonn in the first days of March, Brandt pressed his suit. Playing on Heath's strong pro-European sentiments, he portrayed the crisis as a golden opportunity for the Community, while offering the practical inducement of German monetary backing for the obligations that the UK would incur to defend the pound. The Chancellor proposed to pool reserves, making the very substantial German assets available for support operations. However appealing such a bold venture, representing a quantum jump toward European integration, must have been for Heath, there were overriding, if more mundane, economic considerations that militated against acceptance.

There was the simple question of practicality. The Bank of England and the Treasury joined in one of their rare alliances to advise strongly against committing sterling to a fixed parity. In their judgment, Britain's continuing payments strains would inevitably mean growing pressure against the pound (vis-à-vis the mark and guilder, certainly; perhaps against the French and Belgian francs as well) which could not be resisted through central bank interventions even with an arsenal expanded by deutschemarks. The Bank of England was particularly forceful in pointing out the futile, costly and possibly unsettling nature of such an undertaking. Furthermore, British membership in the snake would deny her the advantages of future devaluations which, in the light of gloomy payments prospects, should be maintained as an option to provide as much flexibility as possible.

These estimates of the proposal's unfeasibility and unproductiveness were shared by the Bundesbank, which formed with the Bank of England a mild central bank lobby. Unenthusiastic about the joint float in any circumstances, Bundesbank officials were adamant in opposing the commitment of German reserves to intervene, open-endedly, in support of sterling. Indeed, the question was raised as to whether legally the Bundesbank could be constrained to undertake market operations, under orders from the Chancellor, which it believed antithetical to its monetary responsibilities.

In the event, the legal issue was never resolved. In these uncongenial circumstances, the British cabinet decided that to join the snake was, on balance, a dubious proposition. In a speech before the Community economic ministers that was intended as much to take Germany off the hook as to state the British position, Chancellor of the Exchequer Anthony Barber set such extreme conditions for Britain's participation as effectively to kill the idea. He declared that "[w]e must all be prepared to grant support without limit of amount, without conditions, and without obligation for guarantee. . . . Only knowledge that support is unlimited and does not impose impossible burdens on the receiving countries can make this system proof against short-term capital flows of the magnitudes now experienced" [4]. As if these demands were not enough, he went on to say that Britain would first make a preliminary devaluation and reserved the right to later rate changes—after consultation. The snake would have to get along without the UK.

France, among the Community members, was least unhappy about this turn of events [5]. She had herself initially opposed the joint float—above all as augering a premature attempt at monetary union and secondarily because of her principled dislike for the floating rate system that the snake would make practicable. With her partners arrayed against her, and with the handwriting on the wall, the French directed their efforts at inflecting the shape of the snake and the conditions of the float. For France, the snake had its attractive, and its threatening features. By including relatively weak currencies, the appreciation of the Community monies could be contained. Yet, if too weak, the common obligation to their defense could place a strain on reserves stored away for her own purposes. Fixing the franc at too high a point vis-à-vis the mark meant hindering French exports and restricting the advantages of flexibility against the revaluation-prone mark—a not insignificant consideration given that the Federal Republic represents 20 percent of France's export market. But a high fixed rate would maintain the absolute level of German contributions to the Community agriculture fund. Still another factor was the seductive possibility of using the joint float as the vehicle for developing a common position against the U.S. on the upcoming agenda of trade and monetary negotiations. On this, as with other projects for European union, France felt an unavoidable ambivalence. A high degree of concertation was needed to countervail American power. But there could be no assurance that a truly unified policy would always point in the direction France desired—especially now that Germany was unquestionably the strongest member of the Community. On balance, with no viable option, the snake was an acceptable expedient. (French approval was encouraged by two developments—a German declaration of a small 3 percent upvaluation made in the hope of moderating the expected upward pressures that could be expected once the exchanges reopened [6], and the public reminder of Helmut Schmidt that Bonn was prepared to go it alone.)

With the British role decided, and the French resigned to participation, the terms of the joint float were hammered out at a weekend meeting of Finance Ministers convened at the EEC headquarters in Brussels. The exchange markets having been closed until March 18, the Ministers met in the shadow of the as yet unresolved crisis. The meeting has been preceded by a ministerial conference in Paris that Friday at which the United States was pressed hard for assurances that it would cooperate fully in the restoration of exchange stability. Specifically, the Community wanted an American pledge to curb liquidity creation by restraining the growth of the U.S. money supply and to revoke plans for phasing out capital controls in 1974, and, above all, a commitment that the Federal Reserve would reintervene, using swap borrowings, in order to counteract any reappearance of exaggerated pressures on the dollar. The swaps originally had been designed to provide credits to central banks whose currencies were weakening against the dollar—credits which could be used to bolster the threatened currency through official purchases. The U.S. Federal Reserve held relatively small amounts of other major currencies for purchases by it of dollars. With the dollar now in danger, arrangements were proposed that gave the Fed greater access to borrowings of other currencies.

Secretary Schultz, as leader of the American delegation, promised that "careful thought" would be given the Common Market's list of measures, but no definite commitments could be made at that time [7]. He was equally noncommital on the central question of reintervention and expressed optimism that the world monetary system would surmount its present troubles, which he innocently termed "one of the rough spots" in the system's withdrawal from dollar dependency. (In a revealing contrast, Arthur Burns, speaking at the same press conference, referred to a "sense of urgency" and urged that "we . . . stop dilly-dallying" [8]. Although the official American response was not as forthcoming as might have been hoped, it was sufficiently accommodating to satisfy the conditions for proceeding with formation of the snake. Consequently, on March 12, the EEC announced the agreement of "the Six" not to abandon predetermined fixed rates and to let their currencies float together against the dollar within their own band of 2¼ percent. In independent announcements. Sweden, Switzerland and Japan made similar declarations of an intended float of their currencies. The former two, based on their own consultations with the Community, agreed to adhere to the common 2¼ percent band.

The dénouement was at hand. That week, at the invitation of the EEC, a 14 nation monetary conference was convened in Paris at the European headquarters of the IMF (encompassing the group of ten major financial and industrial powers, and Switzerland—invited specially in recognition of her key role in monetary affairs—along with Denmark, Ireland and Luxembourg as Community members). In attendance were both Treasury and central bank representatives. The object was to give shape to the understanding on floating, or, more precisely, to reach a de facto agreement that central banks no longer would be obliged to maintain their currencies at fixed values vis-à-vis the dollar. There was no intention, however, of formalizing the accord by publicly citing flexible exchange rates as the official adjustment mechanism—for two reasons. First, the disarray and uncertainty on the exchanges had reached such an extreme that it was felt prudent to reaffirm the responsibility of governments for international monetary stability, even as currencies were taken off their pegs to remove the temptation of the one way bet. Second, there remained substantial differences of opinion as to the manner and extent of central bank intervention. The main purpose of the communique was to instill enough confidence as to permit reopening of the exchanges while steps were taken to cushion the effects of capital movements. No specific reference could be made, therefore, to the established fact of floating. Instead emphasis was laid on the readiness of authorities to reintervene, with the implication that the market alone would not be allowed to determine the new equilibrium points—wherever they might be.

Given its purposes, and the lack of consensus on particulars, the communique was necessarily vague. It stated that

> the ministers and governors reiterated their determination to ensure jointly an orderly exchange-rate system. . . . They agreed in principle that official intervention in the exchange markets may be useful at appropriate times

> to facilitate the maintenance of orderly conditions. . . . Each nation stated that it will be prepared to intervene at its initiative in its own market, when necessary and desirable, acting in a flexible manner in the light of market conditions. . . . To ensure adequate resources for such interventions, it is envisaged that some of the existing "swap" facilities will be enlarged . . . [9].

The ministers and governors also reaffirmed "their attachment to the basic principles that have governed international economic relations since the last war—the greatest possible freedom for international trade and investment and the avoidance of competitive changes of exchange rates" [9].

The differences in interpreting "orderly conditions" and the "appropriate times" to resume official support operations were soon in evidence. Secretary Schultz, while acknowledging that "we stand prepared on an *ad hoc* basis in consultation with other parties to use intervention where we think it may be helpful," took pains to point out that the U.S. had undertaken no specific commitment except to consult and cooperate [10]. The German government made known its view that intervention was undesirable at this time, and pointless until it became clear how the markets would react and the objective of interventions was clarified. In keeping with what had been France's position that the enunciation of the principle of flexibility should not be an excuse for permitting a sharp drop in the dollar rate, Giscard, for his part, voiced confidence that "our American interlocutors will make their contribution to the defense of parities." He interpreted the failure to set fixed points for central bank interventions as a strategy to outwit speculators by giving them "no clue as to exact official plans" [11].

As for the central banks, most assumed reintervention almost as a matter of course. They inclined to see the agreed extension of swap lines as the logistic contingency planning for the inevitable resumption of war with the speculators. *The Financial Times* commented on this "strong temptation for central banks to treat floating rates as if they were really fixed and to intervene almost as a reflex operation when rates begin to move" [12]. One partial exception was the Bundesbank. There, the respected and influential Deputy-Governor, Dr. Emminger, was an articulate partisan of a genuine free float. In broad agreement was the analysis of the academic theorists that speculation under a floating regime would not produce wildly fluctuating rates but rather would tend to be self-equilibriating. Moreover, in the light of recent sad experience, he judged the possible risks as less worrisome than the manifestly disturbing effects of trying to control the markets through intervention. He was prepared to give floating a fair run. Even at the Bundesbank, though, there was no unanimity of view. The president, Karl Klassen, was far more skeptical of the promised fruits of floating, and soon there would be disagreement with Emminger over when and how to intervene.

Within months these differences in interpretation and preference were to grow into sharp disputes as the new system confronted its first test in the renewed speculative surges of late June and July. For the time being, though, a consensus had been reached, a monetary modus vivendi achieved. A means seemingly had been found for stabilizing the exchange markets, par values had been abandoned and in the process the international monetary system had emerged from the crisis with a new adjustment mechanism—whatever it was.

It had been by a process of elimination that the governments had settled on flexible exchange rates—or their own ambiguous variant thereof. The floating system they conceived was a far cry from the pure model of the free market in currencies propounded by the keener academic advocates of floating. In most official minds, it was a wholly pragmatic step dictated by events. For nearly all central bank directors, the change in exchange mechanisms was only a tactical adjustment in the Bretton Woods system, necessitated by forces beyond their control, that carried little potential for resolving its fundamental difficulties and inherent contradictions. The crisis circumstances in which it was introduced, and the prominence accorded the efforts to deal with highly vivid capital surges, lent a dramatic aura, and thereby implied importance to the measure that was out of proportion to its real significance. It represented for these *cognoscenti* the least undesirable and least unfeasible of the alternatives available. Floating was in the manner of a deus ex machina; or, to change the metaphor, an expedient by which to neutralize the hydra-headed menace of currency speculation that had undermined the credibility of the par value system. However one evaluated the relative importance of the several underlying factors that had so gravely and permanently undercut the viability of fixed rates, very few monetary officials accepted the academic claim that flexible exchange rates in and of themselves were capable of resolving the basic problems. As one central banker explained the move, "floating exchange rates had little attraction for us, we were pushed off fixed rates." In the words of another, the decision was "a course of least resistance, if not a counsel of despair." Critical commentators in the academy have looked upon central bank opposition to floating as stubborn assertion of bureaucratic interests and a liking for the exhilaration of doing monetary battle with speculators. However, whatever excitement officials previously might have felt about their heroic combat to save one of their struggling brethren from an involuntary capitulation in revaluation, it had been dissipated by March 1973. "We could not continue to act as a fire brigade" seemed the consensus among central bank officials—with good reason. Chronic instability on the exchanges—the sloshing of great waves of liquid capital from one currency to another—was defeating their efforts at rational monetary policymaking domestically, putting in question their power and authority.

As an expedient, the logic of floating was eminently simple. The answer to speculation was to terminate the commitment to fixed rates, and with it the obligation of central banks to defend them against market forces. Pegged rates would cease to serve as sitting targets. In principle, each currency would find its level according to the rules of supply and demand in the market place—i.e., its price would be set by private buyers and sellers on the currency exchanges—whether those transactions were to cover commercial trade and investment or to seek short term advantage from interest rate differentials and anticipated rate changes. The central bank of a country with a weak currency (one whose relative value was declining because demand for it did not match the supply of those willing to dispose of it at a given rate) no longer need respond automatically by trying to prop it up. With official support operations curtailed, and with such intervention points as might exist kept obscure, floating seemed to remove temptation from before the covetous eyes of speculators. Currency speculation would be more of a gamble insofar as rate movements were less predictable, and theoretically could move in either direction in response to short term market behavior. Thus the logic of floating seemed capable of solving the immediate problem of disorderly markets.

But a key issue had been left unresolved. Just what was governments' responsibility for maintaining exchange stability, and how were they to go about it? The March accords that called for intervention by monetary authorities when "appropriate" had left for future discussion by the Committee of Twenty and technical groups the task of stipulating criteria for measuring disequilibria and writing guidelines for central bank operations. Would the float be free or managed? Was the operative principle stable but flexible rates or a market-induced equilibrium? Each participant held to its own understanding. The period of "benign irresolution" was brief and the test of conviction in floating not long in coming.

THE JUNE-JULY CRISIS

For a short time—between March and the end of June—rate fluctuations were relatively small and ambiguous in direction and capital movements restrained. Market traders as well as governments were accustoming themselves to the new environment. The last week of June saw this "false peace" shattered by a massive flight from the dollar. Apparently stimulated by the spate of Watergate revelations that cast doubt on the probity of American economic policy, it gained momentum in the now recognizable pattern. Dollar holders, still dubious about the currency's credibility, progressively lost whatever confidence had been restored, and anxiously sought to cut their losses. Without the countervailing force of official support operations, the money markets experienced an unprecedented turbulence, outclassing the old records for volume and pace of capital flows set just three and a half months earlier. Déja vu experiences were recorded everywhere.

The dollar plummeted. It dropped sharply against every other major currency—by a whopping 15 percent, on average. Even the lowly pound found itself the embarrassed recipient of a substantial revaluation. The downward fall seemed to have no bottom. Once again disorder swept the exchanges, threatening a general breakdown. *Le Monde* headlined the "absurdity" of the dollar's inexplicable decline to ludicrously unrealistic depths [13]. *The Times* of London talked ominously of "gadarene surves," creating a "chaotic, uncontrollable situation" [14], while Germany's Secretary for Finance saw evidence of "psychopathology" [15].

The crisis was unlike its predecessors in that the central banks, by refraining from intervention, simply let the volatile market force dramatic changes in exchange rates. The earlier speculations involved placing one way bets on expected official revaluations and speculators made their profits primarily against the central banks. On this occasion, the momentum was generated by growing fears of losses from the downward spiral of the dollar and offered gains to whomever purchased other currencies before the dollar reached an as yet unperceptible floor. A host of self-protective, rational decisions of small dollar-holders produced cumulative irrationality. Even potential profit-takers were deterred as the wave of selling fed on itself. It was an old-fashioned financial panic focused on one currency—the pivotal one. The other fundamental difference between this crisis and its forerunners was that drastic changes were being forced in the comparative values of the other main currencies as the market, left to its own devices, was dutifully recording the sales of dollars in sharply lowered rates. For America's trading partners, there was reason to be disquieted.

French Finance Minister Giscard d'Estaing, with the dollar sinking below four francs, decried the "irrational behavior of the market," and warned that "we will not let a situation be created in which large sectors of the French economy disappear from international competition because the parity of the franc vis-à-vis the dollar is too high" [16]. At a time when preparations were being made for the grand conclave on trade and tariffs scheduled for Tokyo that September, the United States—thanks to this sudden lack of appetite for the dollar—already had had the terms of trade shifted further in its favor than any proposal on the agenda dared contemplate, and more than could be compensated for by any agreement that might be reached.* President Pompidou, viewing with alarm the realization of his worst fears about the consequences of floating, declared that "the United States must decide to defend its own money" [17], while musing ruefully about the pride and integrity of a country that allowed its currency to be debased without moving a reserve to defend it. The Banque de France's Director General, Olivier Wormser, jointed the French chorus in declaring that the international monetary system "is on the reefs; it no longer floats, it must be relaunched" [18].

The West German government, more discreetly, also made known its displeasure with the disorderly state of affairs. Less anxious about the appreciation of the mark that was taking place, it was more upset

*Throughout the spring, the French had persisted in their campaign to make the linkage between exchange rates and talks with the U.S. on commercial questions. Foreign Minister Jobert insisted that the advantage given American exports by the decline of the dollar be acknowledged, if not rectified, before the EEC should proceed to discuss reciprocal reduction of import duties. Unable to persuade his partners to hold participation in the trade negotiations hostage to a resolution of what was to Paris the still outstanding problem of exchange stabilization, he did succeed in inserting into the communique of the EEC Council of Ministers (which stated the Community position) the bland notation that "a policy of trade liberalization cannot be successfully pursued unless joint efforts are made to set up an adequate monetary system" [19]. None of France's fellow members shared her acute sense of commercial vulnerability, and none were not anxious to force a coupling of the two issues. The French linkage strategy, with its vague threat of noncooperation in the Tokyo trade talks, proved difficult to sustain. For the administration in Washington was able to make—and felt no compunction about doing so—its own embracing linkage between economic issues generally and the alliance security system. In oblique retort to French criticisms, Secretaries Kissinger and Schulz raised the ante by reminding whomever might be listening that monetary and commercial matters must take particular notice of the costs incurred by the U.S. in meeting its military obligations to the alliance. A failure to do so would necessitate a review of America's commitments. Jobert soon found it prudent to opt out of this game of escalating linkage bids. Addressing the French Assembly in June, he rejected outright any "global negotiations" between Europe and the U.S.

about the capital surges which they thought themselves spared by the introduction of floating. The Bundesbank remained hesitant, though, about urging massive interventions. There was in fact a rift between, on the one hand, Deputy-Governor Emminger, who was inclined to give the market a chance to right itself and pessimistic about the effectiveness of renewed support operations; and, on the other, President Klassen and the director of market operations, Johannes Tüngler (who, in the organizational setup of the Bundesbank, had a margin of independence for conducting interventions on his own discretion.) As the crisis deepened, the latter view was to prevail and the Bundesbank began to make small dollar purchases. The British, for their part, were already committed to pragmatic intervention. With the pound having risen unnaturally by 13 percent against the dollar, the route for pragmatism to take was unmistakable. The point clearly had been reached where, as a *Times* of London editorial put it, "the uncertainties and illogicalities of the present 'flexible' international regime outweigh the advantages" [21]. One of these illogicalities was adverse trade terms for British goods.

In sharp contrast to European expressions of alarm, the official United States position was to play it cool. In accordance with the prevailing belief that the paramount American interest was to achieve a reduction in the dollar rate and to avoid any firm commitment to defend it at a predetermined point, American spokemen tried to downplay the situation's seriousness. Commerce Secretary Peter Flanigan termed the dollar slide a "modest erosion" [22]. The Chairman of the Council of Economic Advisors, Herbert Stein, saw "no reason to support the dollar" [23]; while American Ambassador Irwin in Paris sought to mollify the French government with the comforting thought that "any effort aimed at defending a rigid exchange rate structure would lead rapidly to disaster" [24].

These conflicting public statements indicated diplomatic stalemate. As the situation deteriorated rapidly, efforts grew to reconcile the Administration to some form of intervention. In Washington, Federal Reserve Chairman Burns took the lead in a campaign to persuade the President that for the U.S. to content itself with the immediate advantages of the dollar decline was dangerously short-sighted. Continued exchange disorder would soon begin to interfere with world trade and could force our partners to engage in competitive dirty floating or provoke retaliatory trade measures. Treasury Secretary Schultz resisted this argument, reiterating that the overriding objective was to rectify the American trade imbalance and stating his continued doubts about the efficacy of intervention and his confidence that the exchange markets would right themselves. Although there were officials in each agency who could be found at any point between the two polarized positions, Burns and Schultz did, on the whole, represent the basic differences of emphasis and approach that continued between the Federal Reserve and the Treasury. The debate was conducted at three levels: one, whether the present crisis was so menacing as to demand immediate American participation in a concerted intervention; two, what was the longer term viability of a floating rate system and the proper role for monetary authorities in regulating it; and, at its most elevated, what was the correct balance to be struck between the perceived American interest and the overall requirements for international monetary stability. In effect, it was an extension and intensification of the disagreements which had divided the protagonists since 1971, now sharpened by the crisis atmosphere. As it turned out, none of the broader policy issues were decided. Expediency prevailed—again.

By July 4 the evidence was undeniable that the dramatic fall of the dollar had created so much uncertainty about money values that the market was drying up. Financial and commercial activity was being frozen while traders waited for a new equilibrium to establish itself. Unless immediate steps were taken to shore up the dollar, the whole system of exchanges could be brought to a standstill. The Federal Reserve's manager of its Open Market Account, Mr. Charles Coombs, had designed a strategy for intervention which had been transmitted by Dr. Burns to the Treasury some days earlier, requesting approval. It had been held in abeyance by Schultz. Now it was decided, on the authority of the White House, that the United States should declare its readiness to participate in a limited intervention, using the swap lines which had been extended in March. Thanks to a fortuitous coincidence, the monthly meeting of the Bank for International Settlements was scheduled that weekend, bringing together officials of the 12 leading central banks (accompanied on this occasion by their Treasury colleagues). Long accustomed to collaborating in similar situations, they had no difficulty in expeditiously arranging the particulars. The task had been facilitated, and the ground prepared, by the regular consultations that had not been abated by the switchover to flexible exchange rates. Although support operations had been suspended since March, central bank officers continued to share the responsibility for monitoring rate movements and capital flows and a continuing obligation to apply those measures of domestic monetary policy—on interest rates, money growth and capital regulations where in force—which had been prominently mentioned in the March communique as necessary adjuncts to floating. With the surges at the end of June came more extensive and urgent communication among the central banks most immediately affected. In the course of this consultation, a good measure of consensus was reached among the directors (and their governors) on the requirements for intervention and among the exchange desk operators on how it should be conducted.

While it probably would be an exaggeration to say that this consultation resulted in an orchestrated lobbying campaign within the several governments concerned, monetary authorities generally agreed on the seriousness of the situation and on the importance of official reintervention. They were performing out of their conviction about the requirements for stability and in their role as guardians of the plus-sum dimension of world monetary relations. It was an agreement that translated itself into a parallelism of advocacy. And when it came time for action at the operational level, Mr. Coombs in New York, Mr. Tüngler in Frankfurt and their counterparts elsewhere were well-prepared to resume support operations.

The formal communiqúe of the Basle meeting signaled, in necessarily stilted language, the reintervention of the central banks. Calling attention to the March 16 accord, "[t]hey [the Ministers and Governors] agreed in principle that official intervention in exchange markets may be useful at appropriate times to facilitate the maintenance of orderly conditions . . ." and then gave the cue to traders by noting that "technical arrangements are in place to implement it" [25]. Simultaneously, the Federal Reserve announced enlargement of the swap lines and, almost immediately, the major central banks moved into the market to support the dollar. Its recovery was predictable. Having dropped far below a level that could be considered economically rational by any reasonable standard, the dollar reacted swiftly to the nudge given it by the central banks. A semblance of order was thus restored to the exchange markets. But it had been achieved through official actions which left even greater ambiguity as to just what was the international monetary system's adjustment mechanism.

NOTES TO CHAPTER 3

1. *Le Monde*, February 23, 1973.
2. *La Stampa*, February 26, 1973.
3. *Financial Times*, March 1, 1973.
4. *The Times* of London, March 5, 1973.
5. *Le Monde*, February 26, 1973.
6. *Le Monde*, March 18, 1973.
7. *Le Monde*, March 20, 1973.
8. *New York Times*, March 17, 1973.

9. *Ibid.*
10. *Financial Times*, March 18, 1973.
11. *Le Monde*, March 17, 1973.
12. *Financial Times*, March 20, 1973.
13. *Le Monde*, July 8, 1973
14. *The Times* of London, July 6, 1973.
15. *The Times* of London, July 5, 1973.
16. *Le Monde*, June 30, 1973.
17. *Le Monde*, July 7, 1973.
18. *Ibid.*
19. *Le Monde*, May 29, 1973.
20. *Le Monde*, June 7, 1973.
21. *The Times* of London, July 6, 1973.
22. *The Times* of London, July 7, 1973.
23. *Le Monde*, July 8, 1973.
24. *Le Monde*, July 10, 1973.
25. *The Times* of London, July 9, 1973.

Chapter 4

The Theory and Practice of Flexible Exchange Rates

The one clear conclusion to be drawn from the July crisis was that a pure float was out of the question. For skeptics of floating, it was the confirming evidence that the speculations which had bedeviled monetary authorities for a decade could not be transmuted into something that was systemically stabilizing by the alchemy of flexible exchange rates. Even those officials most sympathetic to FERs (whether out of intellectual conviction or estimation of the benefits to be gained from floating) were forced to accept the responsibility of at least selective intervention. While it might be, as many of the academic supporters of floating claimed, that the disorders were a transitory phenomenon and only to be expected as the markets sorted themselves out, the stakes were too high for indulging the curiosity to find out. Most officials lacked both the gambling spirit and appreciation for the existential joy of living with indeterminancy to permit a system in which they simply accepted whatever rates the exchange markets registered. (It was, in the words of one central banker, like driving down a dark country road at night without lights, never knowing when you were going to hit something.) With the capitulation of the Administration in Washington and the Bundesbank, the option of an unmanaged free float was discarded. The now inevitable managed float was, as one observor noted, "nothing but the expression of [the] discrepancy between reality and the conditions required for the effective operation of an ideal world" [1].

However expedient an innovation, FERs did represent a major transformation in the thinking of monetary authorities. Fixed rates were the keystone of the Bretton Woods system. They had been viewed as the absolutely crucial, unchanging points of reference for national policymakers and private actors alike [2]. Official opinion had accepted with near unanimity the argument of the IMF report of December 1970 on *The Role of Exchange Rates in the Adjustment of International Payments* that "the basic principles of the Bretton Woods system were sound, and the par value system provides a framework for the maintenance of stability and order in exchange rates which is an essential condition for the expansion and balanced growth of international trade" [3]. As late as the mid-1960s, as one participant-observor has commented, "open-minded official consideration of greater exchange rate flexibility was not only not on, but the subject was essentially taboo" [4]. Reality has a way of intruding, though, on the thinking of governments (and, occasionally, on that of theorists as well). The viability of the par value system, and the credibility of monetary authorities, had been steadily eroded by recurrent crises.

The first bubble of interest in FERs had surfaced during the gold crisis of November 1968, only to subside with its resolution. This pattern repeated itself intermittently during the following troubled years, and on each successive occasion the idea of floating gained a little more respectability. When the change came, however, it was more by inadvertence than design. The advent of generalized floating in March 1973 happened without either prior plans for how it would work or technical agreement on the economic principles and analyses that underlay the case for it. Officials were learning how to work the new system by a process of trial and error. In the process governments—as well as economists—were learning a good deal about the modern international economy.

THE THEORY

In the Introduction we spoke in general terms about the way governments—and individuals, too—respond to adversity and about the problem of innovation. Our discussion stressed the natural conservatism of thought and action. The first instinct is to reassert conventional ideas and manners of doing things. There is a parsimony of critical self-consciousness; central beliefs are changed last. Ideas and interests—whether national, organizational or personal—have a strong affinity for those doctrines and theories which protect them and confirm their worth. Pragmatic, step-by-step adjustment is the hallmark of the process of change.

These tendencies were readily apparent in official responses to the exchange crisis. They also give us a clue as to the relationship between the governmental consideration of flexible exchange rates and the lively academic debate that had run through the world of monetary economics for more than a decade [5]. By the usually temperate standards of the profession, it evoked intellectual encounters of rare passion and exhortation, engaging the minds and, sporadically, the amateur political talents of a wide array of scholarly luminaries [6]. The exchange rate issue was for international monetary economists what the counterforce versus finite deterrence doctrinal standoff has been for strategic nuclear analysts (and also shows promise of a similar phoenix-like quality). The issue's central place in academic discourse accurately reflected the critical importance of the adjustment mechanism in the real world of commercial and financial transactions.

The interchange between theoreticians and practitioners had three notable features:

1. government officials were prone to narrow the issues and to simplify exposition of them (even when by professional background they were quite able to deal with analytical questions in their full complexity);
2. there was a demonstrable tendency among officials to place selective emphasis on those interpretations, analyses and prescriptions most pertinent to their own priority concerns and to be inclined toward those models which suited their own philosophical predilections;
3. a strong preference was demonstrated for making practical judgments and offering recommendations that fit technical analyses to established institutional and procedural formats.

In theory, a system of freely floating exchange rates has a captivating simplicity. Instead of constantly struggling against the capital markets to maintain par values, the "natural" forces of supply and demand govern the price of currencies. Normal speculation clears the foreign exchange markets, automatically adjusting the rate structure. These rates will be more in keeping with real economic forces than ones arbitrarily set by monetary officials lacking the necessary information and tools to make confident (and correct) judgments as to proper equilibrium points—and to remake them continually as the multitude of factors in the exchange equation shift.

As its more doctrinaire advocates had it, floating was more than a device for extricating central banks from the impossible position of trying to defend untenable par values. Payments disequilibria themselves would cease to exist. A country's incipient deficit would lower its currency's exchange rate, thereby (1) assuring a spurt in exports and an accompanying drop in imports and (2) attracting investment funds (according to the tenets of orthodox economic theory). In this way, a homeostatic balancing of external payments would operate. Tautologically, the ancillary problem of having to take unwelcome domestic action to adjust for payments imbalances would also disappear [7]. A government no longer would be faced with the intolerable choices of putting the screws on its economy *or* forcing a devaluation (with the threat of possible retaliation from competitors and uncertainty as to whether it was too large or too small to achieve its intended purposes) *or* arranging deficit financing. Consequently, monetary and financial policy would be freed from their bondage to exogenous forces.

Professor Fritz Machlup, a doyen of international monetary economists, was one among the leading theoretical apostles of flexible exchange rates who confidently predicted that floating would bring an end to chronic payments imbalances and exchange instability. As he saw it, "Under a system of greater flexibility such serious disalignments of exchange rates would never, or hardly ever, arise, and expectations of change would be confined to miniscule adjustments" [8]. Thus, he argued "the introduction of freely floating exchange rates . . . would relieve central banks once and for all of any function in the international payments system" [9]. Indeed, since there would be no reason to intervene in the money markets and no need for intervention currencies, and since the covering of debts out of available reserves would no longer be necessary now that payments disequilibria would be adjusted through self-regulated shifts in exchange rates, then the new arrangement also "would remove any requirement to hold reserves for foreign payments." Machlup was given forceful backing by Milton Friedman, who claimed with his usual definitiveness that "a system of floating exchange rates completely eliminates the balance-of-payments problem" [10]. A currency's price may fluctuate, but there cannot be a deficit or a surplus threatening an exchange crisis.

For the more expansive advocates of floating, FERs would be the keystone in a fundamental reconstruction that would substitute the free market for government action in regulating exchange transactions and adjusting payments balances. To these staunch believers in the greater efficiency of the market mechanism, not the least of FERs' attractions would be the drastic diminution of central banks' international role—a prospect that the former regarded as an unalloyed benefit for monetary health and stability.

Relatively few supporters of flexible exchange rates shared this unqualified faith in the dramatic curative powers of floating. They were more modest in their claims and cautious in their expectations. A favorable attitude toward floating followed logically from a rejection of the old par value system as unworkable and a source of constant disruption. But there was wide disagreement within the profession as to just how the various parts of the international monetary system fit together (leaving aside the self-willed governmental parts) and therefore a variety of viewpoints as to exactly what floating would do.

Contention centered, in the first instance, on the question of *whether unregulated speculation would be stabilizing or destabilizing.* The more doctrinaire free market advocates argued that "speculation has generally been clearly stabilizing" [11]. Speculative capital is only destructive, they argued, when it breaks through the contrived dams of fixed rates mistakenly constructed to contain it. Fears of wild, random movements were seen as unwarranted. To those who worried about the capricious consequences of floating, Professor Machlup advised that "[i]t pays to liberate oneself from such myopia and to recognize that speculative capital movements are in most cases only the outward manifestations of a rather durable disequilibrium in commercial trade" [12]. At those times when speculation pushes a currency beyond what objectively would be a reasonable equilibrium point, the normal market tendency would be for countervailing forces to contain excessive swings. Profit taking and opportunity buying would assure a restabilization.

Clearly the exchange markets did not function in this self-equilibriating manner during the period of free floating in the spring of 1973. FER advocates predictably described the turmoil of June-July as the sorting out process of markets distorted by years of official management (or mismanagement). Others—academic skeptics of a pure float and monetary authorities—saw the disorders as striking testimony to the dangers inherent in unregulated currency markets. Some of the latter foresaw the exchanges being infected with the psychology of the stock market. While the stock market's nominal purpose is to generate capital for corporate investment (and arbitrate competing demands for capital), in practice transactions have a low correlation with the performance of firms whose shares are quoted. Rather they are keyed to hopes for gains from short term ups and downs in prices. Similarly, the purpose of the exchange market is to enable those who conduct business across national boundaries to acquire the several currencies that serve as media of exchange in their areas of operation in accordance with need—present and prospective. The fear of those who employed the stock market analogy was that the hopes of making a killing by anticipating short run rate movements (or forcing such a movement) could easily distort those rates and in anxious circumstances provoke quite drastic fluctuations.

Some central bank officials took particular pleasure in using the June-July panic to discredit the more passionate supporters of a pure float. The theoreticians' sanguine view of speculation was taken as the naive optimism of market theorists unschooled in the ways of the currency markets and unpracticed in the art of dealing with them. They were criticized for their faith that rationality is as the market does and for making their characteristic error of reifying the idea of a pure market distinguished by strict individual rationality and uncorrupted by the presence of dominating actors. As most central bank officials saw it, there was no empirical ground for the belief that the divine hand of the market could transform a myriad of individual self-interested actions into a systemically stable outcome. For one thing, the tolerances for erratic or extreme shifts are much finer in the international money market than elsewhere—what is changing is not the price of goods, or financial paper, but the value of money itself. Moreover, given the thinness of the currency market and the concentration of the largest sums of mobile capital in the hands of relatively few actors—banks, multinational corporations, wealthy private holders of Eurodollars (and now the oil states)—comparatively few decisions to buy or sell a particular currency could create sufficient impetus to stir holders of a menaced currency to succumb to a bandwagon psychology and to seek protection against an acceleration of the trend by selling. It would create a classic situation of self-confirming behavior. For this reason, an unmanaged float was seen by most monetary authorities as "exaggerating the effects of speculative capital movements," rather than containing them [13].*

A second, and closely related, question regarding the disturbances that might be encountered under a flexible rate regime was *whether constant oscillations in rates induced by short term currency trading would interfere with international commerce.* Wide and erratic fluctuations conceivably could create so much uncertainty, and so distort the terms of trade, as to hamper the normal conduct of business. Evaluations of this danger depended on two judgments: (1) How much rate fluctuation would there be?; and (2) How adaptable are the forward markets to cover exchange risk?

In practice the markets have been highly volatile, despite heavy

*As Professor Ronald McKinnon has commented, looking back at this debate, it was never made clear "who was to be a stabilizing speculator and what would be the source of private capital for such a speculation . . . and whether it would be forthcoming on the huge scale needed" [14].

management by the central banks. Movements of 2 percent in one day and of up to 5 percent in a week—often reversing themselves over a longer period—have occurred. In spite of these gyrating rates, international trade has contrived to expand nicely, slowing only with the onset of the recession in late 1974. Forward markets, contrary to the fears of skeptics, have worked smoothly, and there has been slight reluctance to assume the risk of taking open positions.** This point of the exchange rate debate has not been entirely resolved though. For it has been argued with seeming logic that until very recently a prosperous, inflationary business environment cushioned the effects of fluctuating rates. In a period of rapidly rising prices when the demand for goods is strong, "the higher costs of international business that stem from large rate fluctuations are passed on relatively easily. In a less inflationary [and prosperous] environment, such higher costs could well prove burdensome enough to hamper international business" [15]—especially smaller firms with limited assets and a more constricted cash flow.

The rather technical debate about the adaptability of forward markets is but one element in a more basic argument as to *whether floating rates in fact are capable of adjusting payments disequilibria.* If they were, then floating would remove the main cause of monetary instability. If they were not, then flexible exchange rates were indeed little more than a palliative for exchange disorder—that, admittedly, a not insignificant role in itself. We cited above the claim of committed FER advocates that rate changes occurring in response to payments imbalances will provide an automatic correction by shifting the terms of trade and directing investment capital in favor of the deficit economy. Hence, floating rates acting as sensitive barometers of economic competitiveness and profit opportunity would assure payments equilibrium. Incorporated in this simplified analysis are a host of mutually reinforcing estimates about economic institutions and economic behavior.

Two are most critical: first, that capital movements and trade flows parallel each other; and second, that trade is highly elastic—that is, demand is sensitive to price differentials and supply to demand stimulation. On the former issue, if the capital account and the current (trade) account move in tandem, then the changes in rates would be both gradual and conducive to the adjustment of payments imbalances. If, however, capital movements have a life of their

**Collapse of the Herstatt Bank in Germany, and significant losses incurred by other banks speculating in currency, did have a chilling effect on financial transactions. However, the decisive action of monetary authorities to prevent the effects from ramifying internationally, and the new caution instilled at the exchange desks, appears to have restored confidence.

own, the terms of trade would be routinely altered without regard to comparative costs and prices—as reflected in export-import balances. Accepting the latter proposition, the IMF reflected prevailing central bank thinking in calling attention to the "risk that countries would find their competitive position subjected to sudden and inappropriate change, as a result of temporary market developments" [16]. Moreover, were capital flows only loosely related to trade performance, then it could be expected that shifts in exchange rates routinely would overshoot equilibrium points, placing further strains on payments adjustment.

The degree of concern with which a government official envisaged a situation wherein capital movements dictated trade terms depended in good measure on how his country might be affected by such a development. Interpretations of how the world operates always stand in proximate relationship to one's objectives in it. U.S. Treasury officials who expected continued deficits on the capital account to pull down the dollar and thereby benefit American exports were inclined to downplay the chances of "inappropriate" rate changes. Officials elsewhere, who would find themselves on the other side of the dollar decline, drew the danger more starkly and used it to bolster their argument about the importance of renewed intervention to keep rates reasonable and stable. Similar disagreements arose in evaluating the desirability of permitting changes in the current account balance to bear the full burden of payments adjustment—as encouraged by a floating rate regime. At the U.S. Treasury there was evident sympathy for that idea. In contrast, America's trading partners—France most vocal among them—saw in this scenario an insidious exploitation of floating to secure for the United States a permanent trade surplus that would perpetuate the exorbitant privilege of the dollar. Not for the first time, in the French view, would the Anglo-Saxon enunciation of an enlightened principle—a free market in exchange dealings—and abstract theory cloak selfish motives.

The *elasticity* question is a key element in the debate about the connection between the trade and capital accounts. It also has a theoretical and practical significance of its own. If modern economies are characterized by high elasticity, then "inappropriate" rate changes induced by capital flows could have a profoundly distorting effect on the allocation of resources—domestically and internationally. However, if demand and supply in international commerce are relatively impervious to rate changes, the danger would be lessened. But the further implication would be that even if the trade and capital account shifted together, the resulting changes in currency values would not necessarily result in payments adjustment.

There was near unanimity among academics and practitioners on the elasticity issue—a phenomenon so rare that it should in itself have aroused suspicion about the correctness of the proposition. Both conventional economic theory and entrenched practical wisdom have held that exchange rate changes have a direct, powerful impact on trade balances. After all, the beneficial payments effect of a devaluation long has stood as an axiom of policymaking. The cautions that were penned in the margins of economic theorizing have, in the light of recent experience, acquired a new significance. The positions of elasticity "optimists" and elasticity "pessimists" are worth reviewing—high elasticity evoking optimism presumably because it suggests that there is some discernible logic to economic performance and an element of truth to classic economic theory.

The predominant view has been that "relatively small changes in the exchange rates . . . should have a prompt effect on the values of imports and exports and . . . should be sufficient, after a lapse of time, to eliminate quite large deficits and surpluses in payments." This is because the "consequences of product cost structure among countries is that international trade flows become much more sensitive to relatively small changes in incomes, costs, prices, and exchange rates" [17]. Critics, though, have begun to detect a number of factors that appreciably reduce elasticity on both the demand and supply side. One, traditional buyer-seller relationships often develop (especially for heavy capital equipment) based on a complementarity with equipment already in place, punctilious adherence to delivery dates, provision of technical assistance, or cultural or linguistic affinities. The first three help to explain the extraordinary resilience of German exports. Two, the ologopolistic organization of a particular industry across national boundaries—cartelization—produces market-sharing arrangements relatively impervious to price changes or, as in chemicals, the trading of specialties. Similarly, multinational businesses often have the power to control supply and to administer prices in order to service existing markets and plants, as well as a desire to maintain political credit in its several host countries. Three, for some commodities—e.g., oil or, increasingly, agricultural commodities—which represent a fair portion of a country's trade, demand is relatively inflexible. Four, the advantages of research and development or scale production in a given industry (aircraft engineering, for example) can be so great as to offset the effects of even substantial rate changes. Five, for another class of goods—namely, armaments—price very often is a secondary consideration. Weapons are a currency of diplomatic transaction to which a monetary cost is attached mainly as a statement of their worth and political significance. Price is not routinely traded off against quality; it is administered through production and export subsidies.

Finally, there are also aspects of domestic economic institutions that restrict elasticity on the supply side. An uncompetitive, inefficient structure of industry; managerial sloth and labor immobility; the wage pressure of well-organized and aggressive unions; and a government reluctance to sacrifice a domestically oriented business to an export-oriented one—all of these factors can go a long way toward neutralizing the effects of a revaluation. More specifically, an industry benefiting from increased foreign sales might soon find its profits the target of workers' wage claims that could swiftly erase the price advantage acquired through devaluation. In addition, where a major devaluation augers an overall austerity program, symbolized by the sharp rise in the cost of imported goods, consumers perceiving a drop in their standard of living might be inspired to reinvigorated efforts at maintaining their position, thereby accentuating inflationary forces and discouraging the investment capital that might have been attracted by the prospect of an export-led boom.

If elasticity "pessimists" are correct, that for these several reasons a rate change will not readily result in payments adjustment, it follows that there would be new temptation to revert to direct control on trade. Import duties and export subsidies have the dual attraction of obviating the need for a restriction of domestic demand while avoiding the costs of imported inflation associated with a currency depreciation. The latent danger of trade wars has been a constant fear (as yet unrealized) in today's unsettled conditions—flexible exchange rates notwithstanding.

Another issue of contention in the debate over floating was the *greater freedom for domestic policymaking* they promised. This was a matter of supreme importance to the economic managers of national governments. Proponents of floating placed considerable stress on relieving domestic policy of the payments constraints imposed by a fixed rate system. As succinctly stated by Harry Johnson, "the fundamental argument for flexible exchange rates is that they would allow countries autonomy with respect to their use of monetary, fiscal and other policy instruments" [18]. For a chronic deficit country like Britain, the prospect of freedom from the importuning voices of trading partners and international bureaucrats was at least as great an attraction as the new latitude in addressing internal problems. They certainly were keen to avoid the restrictive aggregate demand policies called for by economic orthodoxy. For its part, a chronic surplus country such as Germany, which saw its most valiant efforts at fighting inflation undermined by the influx of speculative capital, also found the idea appealing.

Critics of the case made in the name of autonomy saw another side to the same reality. They were quick to point out that floating removes the balance of payments discipline from governments already loath to inhibit expansionary policies. As a consequence, trading and financial partners might find *their* internal policies affected by undesired rate changes as the debtor went his profligate way. As IMF Managing Director Johannes Witteveen has commented, "governments, especially democratic ones, are prone to pursue expansionary policies and . . . exchange flexibility removes the inhibitions formerly imposed on this tendency by fear of running out of reserves and of incurring the political odium of devaluation" [19]. The same safety valve of automatic rate adjustment that conveniently relieves the pressure for domestic constraint is at the same time tolerant of excesses.

Under floating, the argument continued, payments balances cease to serve as an indicator of the need to take corrective action. One country's free-wheeling policies will ramify throughout the system. Rate changes resulting from government A's monetary and fiscal policies impinge on government B's power to make its policy with confidence that the ground will not be cut from under it by sudden rate movements with attendant effects on internal prices and money supply. As Marina Whitman has summarized the problem with reference to monetary independence: "[W]hile rate flexibility endows a country with greater control over the nominal money supply, to the extent that there are feedbacks from changes in the exchange rate to the domestic price level, the real money supply remains an endogenous variable rather than a policy variable subject to the control of domestic monetary authorities" [20].*

Winning control over the internal money supply, we should recall, was the primary attraction of floating to inflation-anxious governments. For the West Germans, inflation was the key to their thinking about adjustment procedures. One of the most hotly argued questions in the whole debate over FERs is *whether floating moderates or accentuates the international transmission of inflation.* An exceedingly complex issue, on which theorists and officials both find themselves clutching at models, it remains highly controversial.

Most supporters of floating accepted, and provided analytical

*Secretary of the Treasury William Simon has made the case for floating partly on the grounds of monetary pluralism. As he told the IMF Governors: "We do not propose to object if foreign countries elect to establish fixed exchange rates among themselves . . . the essence of a voluntary system is to permit free choice—so long as our desire for essential freedom of the dollar exchange rate is respected" [21]. What he neglected to mention was that other countries are denied the choice of fixing their currency vis-à-vis the dollar by the American use of its freedom to float.

backing for, the position of German monetary officials that the fixed rate regime was unduly tolerant of inflationary domestic policies and placed inflationary pressures on more prudent governments. The unwillingness of deficit countries to deflate meant that surplus countries were confronted by inflationary demand pressures; that the formers' chronic payments imbalances will expand international liquidity, large portions of which will seek refuge in the hard currencies of the latter, thereby upsetting domestic money management. Floating promised to cool money movements, curb inordinately large surpluses and remove the exogenous influence on internal money supply and price levels.

The skeptical view of inflation under floating questioned the notion that flexible exchange rates in practice would provide this insulation and argued that a flexible rate regime would give rise to new, serious sources of world inflation. One, by removing whatever payments discipline existed on inflationary policies, a continuation of unfettered expansion would be assured. In the first instance, it is argued, the new regime tends to "concentrate and magnify inflation in the countries in which it originates" [22] (as poor export performance lowers the exchange rate and increases the cost of imports). The tendency under floating alluded to earlier for depreciating currencies to overshoot their equilibrium points would accentuate this inflationary pattern.

On a global scale, the price effects might balance out if "countries whose currencies are appreciating experienced fully offsetting deflationary pressures." However, as Alfred Hayes, former president of the Federal Reserve Bank of New York, has written, since today's economies

> have price and cost structures that are by and large not as flexible downward [and since factor mobility is imperfect], these offsetting movements do not occur. . . . This asymetrical behavior between appreciating and depreciating countries at one point in time can also be expected to occur in an individual country over a period of time, as its exchange rate moves up and down. Following a depreciation, costs and prices will go up. Following an appreciation, however, its costs and prices cannot be expected to decline significantly, and certainly not by the full amount of the previous increases. With excessive rate flexibility, we could thus have a "ratchet" effect that could become a strong inflationary force in its own right" [24].

Either arbitrary and oscillating rate movements or overshooting rate adjustments would accentuate inflation in this way.

The gist of the economic argument about downward price inflexibility is that these days there is no natural or equilibrium price level that anchors money values. Adjustment of costs and prices depends, first, on "money illusion," which is the idea that people do not distinguish a real change in money incomes from a paper change. This proposition is simply no longer valid since the public is too savvy about money to confuse purchasing power with nominal wealth. The second dubious assumption about price flexibility is that business will try to exploit a cost advantage—e.g., as an exporter in a country whose currency undergoes depreciation—or pass on to buyers a drop in costs—e.g., an importer in a country whose currency has been upvalued. There is growing evidence that neither proposition can be sustained. On the contrary, price indexes tend to move in step across national boundaries. It is this phenomenon that is at the core of the argument that flexible exchange rates are on balance inflationary.

GOVERNMENT INTERPRETATION

Just how did a particular government or agency official evaluate the differing analyses of economic experts and weigh the pluses and minuses to be expected from floating? Perceptions of national interest were the main determinants, often colored by institutional position. They were not the sole considerations, though. Individual background, philosophy and simply intellectual judgment also had a role to play. However, it is clear that whatever fascination the theoretical puzzles held for the acute and knowledgeable minds of practitioners, they in fact did not treat the questions as parts of a formal intellectual exercise.

Judgments depended very much on a country's peculiar circumstance. Any Treasury official wrestling with the increasingly intractable problems of economic management could not help being drawn to the idea of a currency float by its promise of removing the external bonds from domestic policy. But on closer examination it was evident that only the key currency countries could expect to secure an appreciable measure of true independence. The United States certainly would enjoy the benefits of an unpegged, inconvertible dollar with little to fear from the potential inflationary or commercial implications of rate fluctuations. Germany, having gained surcease from massive capital intrusions, had the commercial strength to overcome even drastic appreciations (and the price stability to contain cost increases). Britain, whose trade and currency were both more vulnerable, nevertheless could anticipate that international sterling payments and deposits would prevent a collapse of the pound, while she availed herself of the new flexibility to deal with the structural defects of her industry with less constricting payments constraints. But smaller countries—even those with strong currencies and superior export performance (the Netherlands, Sweden)—were far more susceptible to external forces. They therefore were more actively concerned about establishing new rules for collective oversight of the international agreements on monetary management and urged as well the harmonization of domestic policies affecting exchange rates and capital flows.

On the outstanding issue of inflation, it is noteworthy that those officials who believed that their economies fared poorly under the old system were more inclined to read the future under FERs optimistically. German monetary authorities struggling unsuccessfully to retain a semblance of control over their internal affairs welcomed the relief from external inflationary forces as expected from floating and were consonantly inclined to assess positively the long term global inflationary trends in the new system. Central bankers elsewhere, as at the Federal Reserve, whose powers of domestic monetary management had been less attenuated, would give greater credence to analyses that forecast an acceleration of inflation.

These convenient alliances of analysis and interest characterize official thinking in policy fields where there are both a large technical component and manifest interests—political or economic—at stake [25]. In the area of international economics there is the complementary tendency to pass selective judgments as to who should respond how to an expected set of conditions. The U.S. Treasury and the Bundesbank were quite prepared to avail themselves, in different ways, of the greater freedom for national policy offered by flexible exchange rates. Yet at the same time they implicitly expected others to observe the discipline which would be stabilizing for the system as a whole (and thereby help create an environment suitable to the achievement of their national ends). Thus, the Bundesbank could make the intellectual evaluation that FERs contributed to collective well-being by relieving the pressure on surplus countries to undertake expansionary policies. But it most definitely was not desirable for a deficit country to use floating as an avoidance device to put off reforms indefinitely. For their part, Treasury officials in Washington looked forward to the pickup in balance of trade that would result from the downward float of the dollar, yet still thought it essential that surplus countries take the measures necessary to reduce exports and encourage imports.

Greater adjustment flexibility could perhaps liberate domestic policy, but the inescapable facts of interdependence assured that a watchful eye would be kept on how the others made use of their freedom.

NOTES TO CHAPTER 4

1. German Council of Economic Experts, *Toward A New Basis for International Monetary Policy* (Princeton, N.J.: Princeton University, International Finance Section, no. 31, August 1971).

2. George N. Halm, "The International Monetary Fund and Flexibility of Exchange Rates," *Special Papers In International Economics*, (Princeton, N.J.: Princeton University, International Finance Section, no. 83, March 1971), p. 12.

3. International Monetary Fund, *The Role of Exchange Rates in the Adjustment of International Payments*, Report of the Executive Directors (Washington, D.C., 1970), p. 67.

4. William Dale, "The International Monetary Fund and Greater Flexibility of Exchange Rates," in C. Fred Bergsten and William C. Tyler, *Leading Issues of International Economic Policy* (Lexington, Mass.: Lexington Books, 1974), p. 7.

5. A sampling of this copious literature would include: *The International Adjustment Mechanism*, Monetary Conference, October 1969, sponsored by The Federal Reserve Bank of Boston; Milton Friedman and Robert V. Roosa, *The Balance of Payments: Free versus Fixed Exchange Rates* (Washington, D.C.: American Enterprise Institute, 1967). Among the papers appearing in Princeton University's respected International Finance Section series, notable are: Ronald I. McKinnon *Monetary Theory and Controlled Flexibility In the Foreign Exchanges* (no. 83, April 1971); The German Council of Economic Experts and Fritz Machlup, *Plans for Reform of the International Monetary System* (no. 3, August 1962). See also Machlup, *The Alignment of Foreign Exchange Rates* (New York: Praeger, 1972), also George N. Halm, ed., *Approaches to Greater Flexibility of Exchange Rates, The Burgenstock Papers*, (Princeton, N.J.: Princeton University Press, 1970).

6. A primary vehicle by which profloating economists sought to persuade monetary authorities of the idea's virtues were the "Burgenstock" seminars organized by Professor Fritz Machlup. From its inception in 1963, the group served as a forum in which officials and academics could exchange theories and practical knowledge on a wide range of monetary issues.

7. Marina Whitman makes this point in "The Payments Adjustment Process and the Exchange-Rate Regime: What Have We Learned?" (Paper presented at the University of Pittsburgh, November 1974), p. 1.

8. Machlup, *The Alignment of Foreign Exchange Rates*, p. 70.

9. Machlup, *Plans for Reform*, p. 51.

10. Milton Friedman and Robert V. Roosa, *The Balance of Payments: Free Versus Fixed Rates* (Washington, D.C.: American Enterprise Institute, 1967), p. 15.

11. Milton Friedman in ibid., p. 21.

12. Machlup, *Plans for Reform*, p. 20.

13. International Monetary Fund, p. 42.

14. McKinnon, p. 6.

15. Alfred Hayes, (former president of the Federal Reserve Bank of New York), "Emerging Arrangement In International Payments—Public and Private" Per Jacobsson Lecture, August 8, 1975, IMF, Washington, D.C.

16. International Monetary Fund, p. 45.

17. Richard Cooper, *The Economics of Interdependence* (New York: McGraw-Hill, 1967), p. 236.

18. Quoted by Kindleberger in *The International Adjustment Mechanism*, p. 93.

19. Johannes Witteveen, Address to the American Economic Association, December 28, 1974.

20. Whitman, p. 17.

21. William Simon, Address delivered September 2, 1975 to the Governors of the IMF, Washington, D.C.

22. Robert Triffin in *The International Adjustment Mechanism*, p. 56.

23. Hayes, pp. 13–14.

24. *Ibid.*

25. Monetary authorities are, for the most part, quite competent to handle the subtleties of scholarly argumentation. Familiarity did not breed contempt as much as agnosticism. It discouraged whatever little inclination there might have been to seek imaginative new answers to acknowledged problems and certainly encouraged officials to use their own discerning judgment in evaluating the case for FERs and interpreting the technical analyses on which it was based.

Chapter 5

Implementing Flexible Exchange Rates

Floating in practice has involved as much uncertainty and controversy as it did in theory. The diverse viewpoints as to the ramifications of flexible exchange rates, the singular difficulty of unraveling the labyrinth of technical issues, the differing assessments made by governments—as well as their divergent purposes—assured that implementation would not be simple or the results readily predictable. The resort to central bank intervention necessitated by the exchange collapse of June–July nailed the lid on the idea of an elegantly simple, painless float.

From the outset, there was an apparent discrepancy between any version of floating exchange rates which had a chance of being implemented and that urged by the more fervent academic advocates. With a few exceptions, monetary authorities bought the prescription, but only to treat one symptom, whereas a complete regime had been recommended. Indeed, the nostrum was accepted only after rejecting a good portion of the diagnosis and adulterating the medicine liberally with old potions. Introducing floating while retaining the option of official support operations represented at once a political compromise and an agnostic position on the main points of scholarly dispute. Looking at this ambiguous outcome of a great academic battle, one participant was led to complain about "the difficulty of determining the efficacy of policies in that after debating alternatives for a long time, authorities tend to do both" [1]. Between the doctrinaire view of the principled pure market champion and the exchange desk officers at the central banks who harbored a preference for the now abandoned par value system—in C.J. Morse's phrase, "the complaisant floater and naive fixed-rater" [2]—were ranged those officials and academics who acknowledged the importance of a modicum of intervention (and harmonization of domestic policy) but did not agree as to the point at which support operations ceased to be a useful rudder in a sea of floating and instead became once again arbitrary price-fixing on behalf of potentially indefensible parities.

The ensuing period has been one of irresolution—a transition toward a still indeterminate future. Noting the heterogeneity of arrangements now in force, an IMF official described a situation in which "we have 10 countries floating with different degrees of intervention; we have 8 countries floating as a bloc, maintaining a very close relationship aming themselves but with no obligation whatsoever to defend a rate with respect to the dollar; and we have 24 countries that have pegged their currencies with respect to the dollar; 14 with respect to the French franc; and 11 with respect to the pound; and we have 53 other countries that have either declared central rates or par values which they defend by intervening in any of the three above-mentioned currencies" [3].

The failure to settle firmly on a new exchange regime is of a piece with the abortive efforts of governments to reach accord on a more comprehensive restructuring of the international monetary system. They are intimately related. The prolonged, and inconclusive, negotiations of the IMF's Committee of Twenty have perpetuated a state of indeterminacy in exchange rates, since clarification of adjustment policy had been linked to its deliberations on other outstanding issues—regulation of liquidity creation, the role of gold and SDRs in reserve balances, procedures for convertibility and national quotas in the IMF [4]. Both the specific task of giving coherence to a flexible exchange rate regime and the wider reform undertaking have been enormously complicated by the severe shocks—the oil price rise and the general recession—which the world economy has suffered since the advent of floating. These two unforeseen, and drastic, developments have added a further measure of uncertainty to world finance while leaving governments leery of new commitments or initiatives.

MANAGED FLOATING

Central bank management of exchange rates today is ad hoc, based on constantly shifting and wholly pragmatic estimates of the market situation. Intervention is situationally determined. With the exception of the European "snake," monetary officials do not follow fixed indicators of equilibrium or intervention points. C.J. Morse, chairman of the Committee of Twenty, has offered a typology of intervention modes according to the degree of central bank management—automatic, prescriptive and discretionary [5]. The participants in the joint Community float engage in presumptive management—i.e., they undertake cooperative support operations when exchange movements appear to threaten to push rates beyond the 2½ percent band they are committed to maintain. Intervention aimed at other currencies—such as the key dollar-sterling-deutschemark rates—are discretionary.

The terms of central bank operations are negotiated for periods of varying duration and are under constant review. There might be informal bilateral coordination (by the Federal Reserve and the Bundesbank to secure the dollar-mark rate); or a more formal grouping in a currency bloc (the snake and its associated currencies—Swiss franc, Swedish and Norwegian kronor); or follow-the-leader relationships (Japanese authorities tying the yen to the dollar); while some interventions are simply unilateral attempts to achieve a desired rate. The common objective has been to assure a basic stability by resisting sudden currency movements and troublesome rate oscillations. This policy of "leaning against the wind" entails routine consultation among the central banks to monitor market developments and to agree on the timing of interventions.

In practice, a de facto "banded crawl" has been established. Monetary authorities in the leading currency countries exhibit a general desire to contain rate changes in keeping with tacit understandings of the implicit zone within which they are trying to limit the changes between their monies. The zone is conceived in relation to the prevailing exchange rate, not with regard to any prescriptive formula for estimating the objectively "right" parities. By keeping the bands obscure and reserving the option of cutting currencies loose altogether when pressures appear too strong to counteract—or when in the prudent judgment of governments they promise a more stable alignment—monetary authorities have sought to have stability with flexibility.

In this way, the Bank of England and the Federal Reserve attempted, throughout 1974 and into 1975, to hold the pound somewhere between 17 and 19 percent below the 1971 Smithsonian peg. However, when in the face of rocketing British inflation and deepening trade deficits, sterling plummeted in December, it was decided to let it fall below the implicit floor. Late that winter, with the dollar in a sharp slide greased by the move toward diversification of petrodollar holdings, sterling rose back through the floor and out the ceiling without being contained. It since has sagged dramatically, on what seems a more reasonable and permanent basis, to about $2. Similar coordinated interventions have been made to stabilize the dollar vis-à-vis the deutschemark. In early October 1974 the dollar went into a nose dive against the mark as a consequence of the adverse reaction to President Ford's outline of his economic program (officials pointed to the withdrawal of some sight deposits of petrofunds as the culprit that triggered the movement). Immediately, the respective directors of market operations, Mr. Coombs and Mr. Tüngler, moved jointly into the market. In this case, the old-style support operation succeeded in stabilizing the rate as desired. It was less successful the following spring when the dollar again dropped sharply, raising the mark close to its zenith of July 1973. The volatile impulses of the currency market have proven difficult to restrain even with renewed central bank intervention.

These joint efforts to contain rate fluctuations were hampered by Washington's continued equivocation about intervention. The Treasury has withheld from the Fed a general authorization to participate in support operations, necessitating considerable circumspection at the Fed as to when, and in what strength, it will enter the market. At the Rambouillet "Economic Summit" in November 1975 some of the restrictions were removed. In principle, routine intervention was sanctioned. Furthermore, detailed, daily consultation in monitoring the exchanges was recommended—a practice not as innovative as the communique implied.

On a regular, more extensive basis, the central banks of the Community countries participating in the snake have acted effectively to keep their currencies within the stipulated bands. That venture suffered a setback in January 1974 when France withdrew from the joint float. Her decision was motivated by the growing disparities of the French and German payments performance, anxiety about anticipated oil deficits and the hope of deriving some export stimulus from a downward float against the mark. A truncated snake—of which the deutschemark was the pivot and which included the strong currencies of Switzerland, the Netherlands and Sweden—was kept alive among members of a northern Europe blood. With an improvement in her payments position, France subsequently rejoined a year later. Unlike the Community snake, and like the understandings with the dollar, the ancillary mark-zone bands were kept obscure so as not to provide potential speculators with a predictable reaction that would recreate the dangers of the one way bet associated with fixed rates.

When exchange management recommenced in July 1973, there was hope in some quarters that it could function with only selective, and relatively limited, intervention. A nudge here, a shove there, interspersed by an occasional adjustment of a new percentage points, it had been hoped, would hold movements down to reasonable proportions. Actually, the central banks have felt obliged to intervene on a large scale, with mixed results. According to some official indications, the overall magnitude of support operations has been greater than under the old system. The volume of transaction totaled approximately $58 billion between July 1973 and January 1975, and continued to increase at a commensurate rate. Of this sum, $1.8 billion represents Federal Reserve sales of the equivalent in deutschemarks, Dutch guilders, Swiss and French francs, and other currencies available through swap lines [6]. The relatively small sums expended by the Federal Reserve reflect a number of factors—early Administration opposition to massive efforts at maintaining a high dollar rate, the preference for having the other central banks take the initiative in intervention and the comparatively heavy trading that was necessary to maintain the snake. The means for extensive support operations are considerable. (The Federal Reserve now has access to swap lines equivalent to more than $20 billion.) Needless to say, this situation is dramatically different from the self-equilibriating model envisaged by the more optimistic champions of FERs and in keeping with the "active" interpretations of the March 1973 communique.

Substantial, and often irregular, rate changes have occurred under the present regime—despite large scale official interventions. The giddy descent of the dollar in July 1973 was followed by a period of relative stability, lasting more than a year, during which the major currencies fluctuated by only a few percentage points. The sense of security, and the renewed faith in monetary institutions thereby engendered, gave to some the impression that the best of both the floating rate and fixed rate worlds had been achieved. The optimism has been short-lived. Several unsettling developments, accentuating payments disequilibria and magnifying short term capital shifts, set off a new round of rate fluctuations in the fall of 1974. First sterling and then the dollar—the two litmus indicators of flux on the exchanges—were pushed through their implicit bands. By February the dollar was belying its earlier strength by sinking 8 percent against the mark, over 15 percent vis-à-vis the Swiss franc, and even appreciating relative to the pound.

In May it plummeted further. The "battered dollar" was then, by nearly all estimates, stunningly undervalued. In less than a year and a half, the dollar had lost 17.6 percent of its value against the DM (35 percent since May 1970); 26 percent against the Swiss franc (45 percent); 17.2 percent against the French franc (27 percent); and 19.7 percent against the guilder. (Weighted against a basket of 16 currencies, the decline was substantially less—6.6 or 9 percent, depending on the exact weightings—because of its relative strength vis-à-vis the yen, sterling and the Canadian dollar.) Two months later, the trend dramatically reversed itself. In July 1975 the dollar rebounded by an average of 10 percent against the major European currencies before stabilizing at levels that were still somewhat below the Smithsonian parities.*

EXCHANGE MANAGEMENT AND DOMESTIC POLICYMAKING

The continuing flux on the exchange markets and the attendant instability of currency values have reaffirmed the central importance of international monetary management just as national governments (and the world community as a whole) confronted the new economic challenge created by oil and the recession. Managers of the domestic economy today are no less attentive to external forces than in 1971 or 1973. Their payments situation bulks at least as large in their view of policy options (the United States partly excepted) and, hence, so do exchange rates. A burgeoning oil bill adds a whole new dimension to the task of achieving equilibrium; disquiet about inflation makes governments as sensitive to an undervaluation of their currency as to its possible overvaluation; and both arouse suspicions about the mercantile intentions of trading and financial competitor/partners. At the same time, central bank authorities are engaged in operations that are more detailed and demanding of discretionary judgment than previously. Managed floating requires the constant attention of monetary officials to rate movements in continually shifting circumstances where little guidance is provided by definitive rules or fixed points of reference. This situation raises the question as to whether the new conditions favor the free exercise of independent decision-making powers by the central banks, whether they militate toward an accentuation of cross-national cooperation and how rate management is integrated into overall economic policy.

Within the central banks attitudes have varied as to what flexible exchange rates demand in the way of regulation and concerted action. It is most often the foreign desk officers who are inclined to

*Constantly shifting rates, moving for unspecifiable reasons, have given a field day to the financial commentators, who now show a weakness for some flighty speculation of their own. In the manner of stock market observors, their only common denominator is the conviction with which even the most bizarre explanations are offered. When the dollar dropped in the spring of 1975, one was treated to commentaries discoursing on the impact of the Mayaguez incident, among other factors. Even more bizarre is the possibility that they were right.

aim for specific equilibrium points and to use the means at their disposal to resist market pressures. Central bank directors, generally speaking, recognize that nowadays an approximation to fixed rates cannot reasonably be the goal. The dominant approach emphasizes the negative objective of avoiding fluctuations and sudden movements. This scaling down of objectives is less a matter of conviction that floating is desirable than an admission that the forces of the market can at best be channeled and not deflected. In practice, the exchange desk officer's freedom varies from country to country. Normally, it is circumscribed by instructions and authorizations, periodically reviewed and updated, that are issued by the central bank's governing board and director. These guidelines might be more or less tightly drawn. In each case, though, they assure that operations will be constantly reviewed by the highest authority within the bank.

In the United States, the Federal Reserve is a firm believer in a carefully managed float. Their view is well represented by Alfred Hayes, the recently retired President of the New York bank. As he states his position:

> My approach is to avoid the wide swings of the kind that we have had in the last 2½ years: not just the bilateral relationships of major currencies that on occasion have exceeded 1 percent, or the weekly swings that have been as high as 5 percent, but also the wide ups and downs of 15 percent or more over the course of a few months. These swings have widely reflected the great uncertainties on the world financial scene that were first set off by the breakdown of the Bretton Woods system and then spurred by the oil crisis. I doubt that such short-term swings serve any economic purpose. . . . My own preferences, therefore, would be to minimize cyclical exchange-rate changes to the extent possible. In summary, I would like to see a firmly managed float that would involve forceful dealing with the market whenever necessary and would allow significant exchange-rate changes only in line with changing fundamentals [7].

This is the approach that, on the whole, has prevailed, despite a quite different attitude at the Treasury. Secretary William Simon has used every occasion (often when reacting to the indefatigable French campaign for a return to fixed rates) to reaffirm his strong conviction that flexible exchange rates are working exceptionally well, that a return to anything like the par value system would be disasterous folly and that intervention is only proper when required to calm disorderly markets (and even at those times should be carefully limited) [8]. These testaments of faith have been coupled with the now familiar comments from the Treasury disparaging the importance of the dollar decline ("the Swiss franc is not the world"), and attributing it to the latent inflationary pressures in the U.S. (at a time when they have dipped below those in Japan and most of Western Europe) [9]. Yet, the Federal Reserve has regained a measure of the operational independence it enjoyed prior to the great crises of 1971 and 1973.

When the Federal Reserve determines that conditions call for support operations and resort to the swap lines, the Fed's Chairman is required by law and custom to inform the Treasury Secretary as to what market operations are planned. During the 1960s, it became the practice for the Treasury to defer to the judgment of monetary authorities intimately familiar with the workings of the increasingly troublesome international money markets. By the end of the decade, as a depreciation of the dollar became official U.S. policy, this tacit grant of independence was gradually withdrawn. It now has been restored to a substantial degree—thanks in part to the Rambouillet accord publicly approving the practice of routine intervention. The Treasury is still informed of any interventions that are being prepared, but the Fed does not have to await explicit approval. The burden of proof has been shifted to the Treasury to raise objections. Despite the very significant fluctuations in the dollar rate, and despite the interventions that have occurred, there appears to have been little inclination to question the actions taken.* In part, this passivity reflects a reversion to the traditional American attitude that exchange rates are not that important since the U.S., as a continental economy, is less affected by them than are other countries. In part, it is satisfaction with the dollar's performance to date. And, perhaps, it is also indicative of a weak Administration preoccupied with more urgent economic matters. Under these conditions the chances for a more active central bank role have been enhanced.

Hypothetically, one could conjecture that central banks are better shielded from political oversight than they were under the fixed rate system. Then, the responsibilities and actions of monetary authorities were, to a large extent, self-defining with regard to exchange interventions. When there was a break in those routine circumstances—i.e., a strong speculative surge or deterioration of a cur-

*The Federal Reserve's operations also receive the careful scrutiny of Congress. The House Committee on Banking, under the chairmanship of Henry Reuss, has been especially vocal in its objection to official defense of what it has viewed as an overvalued dollar. The committee position is compounded of equal parts anxiety about American export industries, dislike for the losses suffered in past interventions and the reasoned preference of its chairman for floating. Here, as in many other areas, Congress has been frustrated in its attempts to bring an executive agency to heel.

rency's position demanding decision on whether to take it off its peg—the attention of central policymaking organs would immediately focus on the problem. Today, with rates constantly shifting, decisions as to the practicality and desirability of resisting, tolerating or encouraging rate changes have to be made constantly. Since oversight can only be intermittent, and primary responsibility lies in the first instance with monetary authorities, the possibility would seem to exist for the more frequent exercise of discretionary central bank judgments.

However reasonable this proposition looks at first glance, there are reasons for believing that the scenario is more theoretical than real. First, the American situation, with its relative indifference to exchange rates, is the exception—and due in some degree to temporary political conditions. It is likely to change when the domestic impact of rate changes becomes apparent (as through imported inflation). Most governments continue to utilize mechanisms of intragovernmental coordination to assure that official actions on the exchanges do not run counter to established policy and that the boundaries for its interpretation are reasonably well defined. Of course, oversight cannot be minute, and a myriad of small decisions can substantially affect exchange conditions. However, the normal responsibilities that central banks feel toward their elected governments minimize the likelihood of their sailing on a tack of their own. Second, until now there has been no serious effort on the part of central banks to calculate systematically what proper and stable rates for their currency should be, taking into account the multiple factors we noted. Their objectives have been incrementally conceived, defined in large measure in reaction to what is taking place on the exchanges. Their cooperation in reaching those targets has an even more pronounced ad hoc quality.

As one connoisseur of exchange rate politics commented in considering the outlook for a deepening of collaboration among monetary authorities, "the so-called long-run is so completely dominated by shorter-term episodes that I am not sure how relevant the long-run considerations are" [10]. The recurrence of episodic mini-crises points up the unavoidable paradox of a situation where the freedom of operational officers is enlarged only so long as conditions limit the impact of its use. Those occasions when drastic rate shifts call for the most extensive cooperation are exactly the moments when superior political authority is likely to assert its prerogatives; while the relatively routine collaboration during calmer periods offers little incentive or scope for expanding cooperation and strengthening joint decisionmaking powers. While flexible exchange rates have substituted a steady tension for the sporadic flare-ups that characterized international monetary life under fixed rates, they as yet do not appear to have altered in any fundamental way the internal governmental arrangements for addressing monetary issues.

IMF INITIATIVES

The International Monetary Fund had been largely bypassed in the switchover to flexible exchange rates. Understandably so, since its Articles of Agreement were predicated on the par value system. One of its main responsibilities was to exercise surveillance over the manner in which member governments met their obligations "to collaborate with the Fund to promote exchange stability" [11], and to raise its importuning voice when it felt that too hasty recourse to revaluation had been made or their internal policies were unsuited to the achievement of payments equilibrium. With the introduction of generalized floating, a key function had been lost, the guidepost for making advisory judgments removed and, thus, the organization's influence diminished. Legally, the fund could not authorize floating except through formal action by its membership. But with floating an established reality, it could attempt to set up ground rules.

The recurrent, and as yet inconclusive, efforts of the IMF to nurture an agreement on the rules for floating are witness to the continuing difficulties faced in trying to give shape to an amorphous reality when national positions and interests differ. The IMF Secretariat, after consultation with members, first took the initiative in June 1974 to propose guidelines. Stressing the imperative need for "a mechanism of international coordination to ensure that the several [national] policies are mutually compatible," they recommended that government intervention should aim "a) to smooth out very short-run fluctuations in market rates; and b) to offer a measure of resistance to market tendencies in the slightly longer run, particularly when they are leading to unduly rapid movements in the rate; and c) . . . to form a reasonable estimate of the medium-term norm for a country's exchange rate, to resist movements in market rates that appear to be deviating substantially from that norm" [12].

The first goal, concerned with erratic day-to-day swings, is the simplest. Agreement on this count is relatively easy to obtain since no government looks with favor on unstable rates and unsettled exchanges. It is quite another matter to achieve the IMF's last mentioned objective. As a technical question, there is no ready formula for making confident estimates of a stable, economically rational equilibrium point accounting for the diverse factors that enter into any calculation of the exchange rate structure. As a political matter, there is little immediate prospect that national governments, feeling the increased strains of oil-induced payments imbalances and always chary of relinquishing their right to act in defense of domestic well-being, will accede to either the authority of an international organization or accept a preprogrammed rate formula. Giscard d'Estaing, as ever most forthright about the national realities behind economic cooperation, stated the dilemma succinctly in declaring that "consultation is necessary and desirable in this field, but it should not lead to delegation of powers or to an abdication of responsibilities by the national political authorities . . ." [13]. As he made clear, "the IMF is only an international institution that has the task of expressing the common will of its member countries. It is a grouping of countries" [14].

Confirming its restricted powers of initiation, the IMF came to terms with the reality of floating in its 1975 Annual Report, while also admitting its inability to write precise guidelines. In effect, the organization gave its blessing to a 30 month interim period of floating. The "experiment" was dictated by the failure of the Fund's governors, at their annual meeting, officially to revise the Articles of Agreement and thereby to legalize the de facto flexible rate regime. While the secretariat report commented favorably on its performance under trying conditions, it found that the lessons learned "cannot readily be translated into precise guidelines for current policy" [15]. The effort to fashion an agreed set of rules received impetus from the informal Rambouillet discussions that went some way toward a reconciliation of the American and French positions. It was that understanding which made possible the agreement at the IMF conference in Jamaica, in January 1976, to revise the Articles of Agreement so as officially to relieve member states from the obligation to maintain par values for their currencies. It remains to be seen whether the Rambouillet accord encouraging central bank consultation and cooperation for keeping currencies within loosely conceived target zones is sufficient basis for successful rate management. Clear criteria still do not exist for distinguishing "erratic and wild" fluctuations (that the meeting decreed warrant intervention) from movements induced by "underlying economic and financial factors" (that should be left untampered with.)

While legalizing a floating rate system, the Jamaican agreement too does not contain explicit rules for intervention. Personal diplomacy has jumped in where formal rule-setters fear to tread. Dr. Witteveen's rounds of the Treasuries and central banks in January 1975 to nurture an agreement on a code of good conduct did help to solidify an implicit understanding that excluded the most egregious forms of self-interested rate management. But they could not be sure that conflicts of national purpose will not give rise to more subtle strategies for influencing the movement of rates. The danger at first perceived in managed floating was subrosa competitive devaluations. Despite the fact that governments hard pressed by huge oil bills undoubtedly have been tempted to compensate for part of their deficit through export drives—spurred by rate reductions—that threat has not materialized. The postwar experience with mutually beneficial cooperation has heightened awareness of the common dangers inherent in reciprocal beggar-thy-neighbor policies. Moreover, the acute concern over inflation has dimmed the attraction of a devaluation that also means higher prices for imports. However diminished, the danger does remain of governments seeking to manage the float to its own advantage. Preventing that occurrence will depend less on specific rules, internationally administered, than on more prosaic forms of intergovernmental cooperation whether stimulated by the IMF or self-motivated. That cooperation has met an unprecedented challenge in the turbulent economic environment ushered in by the oil price rise and worldwide stagflation.

OIL AND STAGFLATION

It has proven singularly difficult to organize the present exchange regime, and equally difficult to assess its workings, because the game has been so drastically changed. The task of designing procedures for correcting payments imbalances and establishing criteria for determining proper equilibrium points among currencies has been enormously complicated by the appearance of some disturbing new elements. The most unsettling has been the threefold increase in oil prices by the OPEC cartel in November 1973. That act added a whole new dimension to payments problems. The consequences are multiple—a dramatic unsettling of external accounts; a quantum jump in international liquidity; aggravation of concurrent recession and inflation.

The most direct result was to throw payments into disarray by shifting tens of billions of dollars into the coffers of the oil producers. The net costs to OECD (Organization For Economic Cooperation and Development) countries for petroleum imports jumped to some $60 billion in 1974, then dropped to an estimated $40 billion the next (recession) year. The most reasonable predictions are that the cumulative surplus will peak at close to $200 billion in 1979 [16]. These costs threatened to push the trade balances of the industrial countries deep into the red. Britain and Italy in particular were confronted with deficits of such magnitude as to exhaust all conventional credit sources. Italy resorted to the extreme measure of import controls—a 60 percent deposit on all import orders—a move that threatened, but fortunately did not set off, a general trade war. France, in somewhat less parlous financial health, was also vulnerable to a sharp downturn in her trade balance and undertook, like Italy, a program of retrenchment. All three countries arranged for large scale borrowing (mostly through their public sector banks and industry) on the Eurodollar market in an attempt to shore up their payments position. This unusual move (in the postwar period at least) did help to tide them over. (It also constituted indirect exchange rate management insofar as borrowing warded off what otherwise would have been a logical depreciation of their currencies.) Germany, alone among major European countries, seemed able to cover the exaggerated costs of petroleum imports thanks to reserves of $35 billion and a still remarkable ability to generate exports. The U.S., less dependent on foreign oil, nonetheless also experienced a $17 billion increase in her oil bill, wiping out what otherwise would have been a substantial $14 billion surplus.*

Monetarily, the most worrisome aspect of the situation was the anticipated *differentials in recycling*. When combined with variations in dependency on petroleum imports and differences in the structure of industry, differential capacities to attract petrocurrencies could not fail to sharpen payments disparities. Since the OPEC countries were able to absorb only a portion (although, as events showed, a surprisingly large portion) of these funds—through purchases of goods and services—the rest necessarily would be reinvested in Western financial markets, either in equity shares, or government bonds and securities, or placed in private banks as short term or time deposits. It seemed evident that a disproportionate share of the

*The improved American balance of trade, which produced a considerable overall payments surplus in 1974 and 1975, has been proclaimed as the long-expected fruits of the cumulative dollar devaluations. A closer look at the figures shows a cloudier picture. The largest part of the turnaround on the current account between 1973 and 1975 is due to the rise in world commodity prices for agricultural products that generated $11 billion in expanded sales. When one adds to this figure a hefty $5 billion increase in arms sales, one finds that these price-insensitive items accounted for over one-half the total gain in exports. It is conceivable that had the dollar remained at its 1970 level, the surplus would have been even greater. Foodstuffs and weapons would have been priced higher and imports lower (oil excepted since its price is quoted in dollars). Thus, the enormous American investment of political capital to achieve its dearly sought right to depreciate the dollar might well have been misdirected, and the ultimate goal of payments equilibrium achieved when depreciation had become superfluous, if not in fact a handicap.

petrocurrency pie would be distributed in a few countries—the U.S., with a market large enough to absorb sums of the projected magnitude; Switzerland and Germany, with their secure currencies; and, to a somewhat lesser extent, the U.K., which benefited from the attraction of London's exceptional financial institutions (as well as the fortuitous fact that many oil contracts are written in sterling).

In 1974, this was the distribution of recycled funds: the United States received approximately 20 percent of all petrocurrencies; the U.K., 12 percent; Eurocurrency institutions took in the largest share, 35 percent (and in the process greatly expanded their pool of liquid capital); with the rest distributed in the form of bilateral loans and obligations to international institutions [17]. Recycling through established financial markets and international programs proved they were able to handle these enormous amounts of capital. But there was little likelihood of their automatically balancing the individual national accounts.

The overriding monetary concern of the industrial nations through the second half of 1974 and into 1975 was the financial consequences of the oil price rise—recycling, in particular. (1974, the Year of the Petrodollar, superseded 1973—The Year of the Exchange Crisis—and preceded 1975—The Year of the Great Recession.) Devising recycling strategies was the dominant activity of monetary officials, and the outstanding issue in the intense trans-Atlantic diplomacy of the period. Two proposals stood highest on the agenda, and constructive action was taken on each. First was the creation of a special loan facility at the IMF, the "Witteveen facility," which would extend long term loans to members suffering severe deficits, using funds subscribed by the oil producers and industrial nations alike. In conception, it was tantamount to an expanded swap agreement entailing medium term borrowing at nonconcessionary (7 percent) rates. Second was the Kissinger Plan, a scheme to form a credit union of industrialized nations. It would pool reserves to backstop any member suffering extreme payments distress and to provide backing for borrowings on private markets.

Differences of opinion about the relative worth and wisdom of the two approaches were a source of considerable contention between the U.S. and the Europeans. Britain, France and Germany all shared a strong preference for going the IMF route. They saw it as the only intergovernmental vehicle that could transfer a substantial portion of the petrocurrency surpluses into the hands—i.e., accounts—of deficit countries. In the eyes of Secretaries Kissinger and Simon, however, the plan had two distinct drawbacks—one, a routinized procedure for providing credit would constitute endorsement of the OPEC prices, which the American government still hoped could be forced down; and, two, IMF voting arrangements, it was feared, were too awkward, and too susceptible to OPEC influence, to perform the sensitive job of recycling. By contrast, the "safety net" would be a Western affair, to be managed in clubby fashion. The Europeans in turn had their reservations about the Kissinger format. Above all, Washington had conceived it as a critical component in their strategy for forging a solid consumer bloc to break the cartel.* Cartel-busting in European eyes was an improbable idea and an exceedingly risky one. On purely economic grounds, sharpest criticism came from West Germany. Bonn was very unhappy with the prospect of putting their hardearned reserves on the line to cover the weak foreign exchange position of their partners. There was also the technical legal question whether the Bundesbank could assume responsibility for the debts of other governments—the same issue that had been raised when Chancellor Brandt proposed to back sterling in a European monetary union.

At the conclusion of protracted discussions, a compromise agreement was reached to implement both plans. The IMF facility (which had been launched some months earlier in embryonic form) was expanded, but its credit bank limited to $6 billion. The Kissinger "safety net" was put in place in essentially the form proposed—after some rhetorical distance was placed between it and Washington's strategy for confronting OPEC. Complementing these initiatives was a European Community plan to establish its own multibillion dollar facility. As planned, the EEC Council would back bonds placed on private financial markets and extend loans from a common fund to members in need. It involves a mutual obligation of its membership to accept responsibility for a defaulting borrower. These new institutions have not as yet been fully tested. As the situation has developed, the danger is less than anticipated.

Anxiety over recycling, which peaked in the winter of 1975, has gradually subsided. OPEC's capacity to absorb goods and services has turned out to be greater than anyone dared hope, while at the same time the deepening recession in the West cut back oil imports sharply, and the combination of private financial markets and specially created borrowing facilities has succeeded in producing a rough balance in the recycling of the surpluses actually in existence. The balancing, however, has not been smooth or exact. Britain has con-

*It was during this period that the American Administration seemed to be taking the curious tack of posing a possible financial collapse of the West as a menace to the OPEC states whose economies would be brought down along with it. The threat lacked something in credibility.

tinued to run heavy deficits despite considerable infusions of petrofunds, deficits that have been covered only through borrowing—in effect, mortgages on North Sea oil. Italy in late 1974 seemed on the verge of default, but managed to pull herself back from the brink through a severe austerity program. France has kept her monetary head above water thanks to retrenchment, loans and an unstinting campaign to arrange barter deals with oil-producing states. Germany's economy has demonstrated the most impressive resiliency. Still riding the wave of her extraordinary export performance, she recorded the improbable record trade surplus of $24 billion in 1974 (a figure trimmed the following year) and attracted substantial petrocurrency deposits. The United States' share of the recycled funds dropped from $12 billion in 1974 to an estimated $5 billion in 1975 [18]. The American payments surplus was generated on the trade account. (American banks did perform an important intermediation function recycling $15 billion into other countries) [19].

Even as the danger of national bankruptcies has faded, unrestrained *growth in international liquidity* has appeared as the new threat to monetary stability. The OPEC nations have placed the greatest part of their surpluses in the Eurocurrency markets. By draining capital from domestic economies, and shifting it into private international financial institutions, they have been creating world liquidity in a completely unplanned and unregulated fashion. Nor is this tendency to place reserves on the money markets restricted to the oil producers—Western industrial nations have also found it convenient to maintain a portion of their reserves on these institutions. The private credit thus created permits deficit countries to borrow in the market, avoiding the need to draw down their own reserves. As Dr. Witteveen has anxiously noted, "these tendencies seem to create a situation where almost any balance of payments disequilibrium could lead to increases in international liquidity" [20]. There is a ratchet effect at work that assures a net growth in liquidity similar to the ratchet effect shifting price levels upward. The oil surpluses have helped ignite a liquidity explosion.

The exchange consequences are twofold. First, the deposit of petrofunds in short term financial instruments has expanded, once again, the volume of potentially disruptive capital at loose in the world. Not only is there increased likelihood of shifting movements forcing rate changes—often arbitrarily—but the prospects are that a comparatively small displacement of funds could trigger the swollen pools of speculative and defensive-minded capital holdings. Moreover, the holders of these new funds are sensitive to political events. The marked decline of OPEC investment in the U.S. in 1975 is explainable as Arab reaction to tough talk from Washington and fear that assets might be frozen in a showdown [21]. The immediate effect was a noticeable weakening in the demand for dollars on international financial markets. In the normal course of events, OPEC has a stake in a sound dollar. The majority of oil contracts have been written in dollars. Its depreciation represented a substantial reduction in the buying power of oil earnings. In the present political circumstance, though, concern about the dollar's value did not engender any attempt to bolster it or slow the move toward diversification. Rather, OPEC decided in June of 1975 to quote prices in SDRs, while continuing to receive payments in dollars. (The practical effect was that if its value declined, more dollars were demanded in payment for a given amount of oil.)

(Some observers have seen a more dramatic threat in the concentration of vast capital funds in OPEC hands—their possible use as a coercive political weapon. To use Fred Bergsten's phrase, "foreign dollar balances are moving from the political allies of the U.S. to its potential political adversaries" [22]. Does Arab wealth really hang like Damocles sword over the financial head of any government whose political stance arouses the ire of Arab oil producers? More specifically, could the sudden withdrawal in sight accounts, and sale of securities, bring about a financial collapse? It is an improbable scenario. On strictly economic grounds, it is impossible to extricate funds without suffering losses, since the initial action immediately depreciates remaining holdings in the target currency. Second, and more critical, the capital would have to be deposited somewhere, and the recipient banks simply could recycle the funds back to the victim. Something of this sort happened in 1967 when a few Arab states moved sterling funds to Switzerland in protest against Britain's perceived pro-Israeli policy. The Swiss redeposited the funds in London banks. Arab financial warfare only becomes credible when they have established an international banking network under their managerial control. Ultimately, of course, the most effective deterrent to financial warfare is the threat of military retaliation.)

INFLATION

The other major development in the world economy, which stands alongside the oil price rise as a cause of exchange instability, is the spread of double digit inflation. Inflation has received some impetus from the increase in fuel costs. Estimates of the cumulative effect on the priced index range between 2 and 6 percent, and the impact varies from country to country. Precise figures are difficult to come by. By pushing costs upward all across the board, the hike in the fuel bill accentuates the spiral of prices (and salaries) as everyone tries to keep up with, or ahead of, a rising cost of living. In this sense, oil has merely given the cycle a few quick spins. An ancillary inflationary effect, which in the long run perhaps will be of greater importance, has been the sharp increase in international liquidity. As we observed, the OPEC surpluses placed on the Eurocurrency market have expanded that portion of the world's money supply beyond the control of national monetary authorities.

These connections seem well established. Inflation as an international phenomenon, though, has had an independent existence of its own, antedating by several years the events of October 1973. Whatever the relative weights one ascribes to its several causes (the exchange rate mechanism among them), it undeniably has had a marked influence on the prices of traded goods, while its unsettling of money values generally creates the kind of unrest witnessed in the early 1970s.

In the first instance, differential inflation rates mean a shift in comparative costs and prices. When Britain experiences a 26 percent per annum increase and Germany a rise of 6 percent, German goods undergo a de facto devaluation of 20 percent (assuming that the quoted prices register the increase in costs). If they do, the price to an American (or Persian Gulf sheik) of an English Jaguar goes up by more than four times the price rise of a Mercedes. Unless the deutschemark floats upward by an equivalent amount (and is permitted to do so), the German trade balance is likely to improve further at the expense of the British, with attendant strains on the latter's payments position and currency.*

Conventional economic theory holds that differences in the inflation rate of this magnitude should profoundly alter trade patterns. One of the most striking features of the present period is that they have not. It is attributable in some degree to the compensatory effect of floating exchange rates. But they are not the whole story, since rate movements are not that closely correlated with price indexes. Until July 1975, the dollar-sterling rate was little changed from fall

*The monetary debates of the midsixties, which were agitated by the relatively mild inflations of 5 or 6 percent (differentials of 3 to 4 percent), marginal payments imbalances and proposed devaluations of 8 percent (the "shocking" American demand at the Smithsonian), seem curiously overdone and rather cosy when viewed from today's perspective—and the problems faced then relatively manageable. In the post–oil price rise, high inflation period, when currencies can fluctuate by 10 percent in a couple of weeks, revaluations of up to 40 percent can be absorbed painlessly (for example, the mark vis-à-vis the dollar) and inflation rate spreads can reach 20 percent, the earlier attribution of great importance to relatively minor changes seems out of all proportion to their actual significance.

1972 despite inflation differentials totaling over 30 percent. Yet the trade shifts were marginal; American goods did not replace British goods on competitive markets on a massive scale. The reason is the type of trade inelasticities we mentioned earlier. Much commerce is price-insensitive. Furthermore, in the modern economy, prices in the international market tend to even out [23]. Higher prices for one country's exports will pull others to its level. The properties of the system that tie prices together are the same ones that obviate the effects of devaluations—inflexibility on the downward side of costs and prices.

Although inflation has not been that disturbing of commerce, official worries about inflation have significantly influenced governments' attitudes toward exchange rates and the criteria according to which monetary authorities intervene on the exchanges. Concern about the inflationary consequences of a currency depreciation now matches interest in its expected beneficial effects on exports and employment. This consideration explains in part why the predicted competitive devaluations never came to pass. As simply put by Marina Whitman, "the twin concerns of stagflation have brought about a certain symmetry in the pressures for depreciation to alleviate unemployment and for appreciation to alleviate domestic inflation" [24]. Stagflation, the current dilemma for domestic policymakers, thus creates a quandry for exchange policy—with officials hard pressed to figure out exactly where their interest lies, much less able to achieve an optimal rate. Conflicts of national interest are muted thanks to the uncertainty as to what those interests are.

The calculation of a preferred exchange rate is complicated by the prominence of oil in the calculus of exchange costs and benefits. Given the relatively inelastic demand for the fuel, a depreciated currency assures a high import bill (with its promise of inflationary pressure and payments difficulties) without any guarantee of an offsetting boost in exports to a depressed world economy. Burdened by these unescapable fuel costs, the industrial nations feel their freedom of action increasingly constricted by inflationary and payments strains. The preferred strategy for each is to have others take the lead in initiating expansion, thereby promoting a world recovery. A recovery led by export industries makes it that much easier to contain domestic demand. Just such strategies were in full flower at the IMF annual meeting in September 1975. The United States, Germany and Japan were offered in turn the honor of being the first to heat up its economy. While objectively their inflation and payments situation made them the most appropriate candidates, each found reasons for demurring.

The consequence of these equivocal policies has been an ambivalent approach toward exchange rate management. Given the subjective uncertainty governments feel about the economic situation, as well as the objective uncertainties of an unstable situation, it is understandable that central banks should find themselves relatively unencumbered by specific instructions from political superiors. The array of often elusive factors that would have to be incorporated in any estimate of an optimal exchange rate is also good reason for monetary officials to set themselves the more modest goal of maintaining a modicum of rate stability. That objective, rather than a specific set of equilibrium rates, is also the basis for cooperative exchange management.

FLOATING—THE BALANCE SHEET

Any overall assessment of the flexible exchange rate regime must be tentative, and hedged about with qualifications. It is not even easy to depict the system. In part, it is a managed float—where the guidelines are constantly changing—in part, an arrangement of fixed but adjustable rates. In one sense, an aggregation of currency blocs; in another, still revolving around the dollar. It defies simple representation. The regime's performance is equally daunting of evaluation. For one thing, the world economy is not what is was in 1973. The oil price hike, the shift of substantial financial power to OPEC, rampant inflation coupled with the deepest recession since the 1930s—all have converged to create conditions drastically different from those prevailing through most of the orderly postwar era.

In this situation, the one conclusion that can be stated with some confidence is that the old fixed rate system could not have handled these developments and that flexible rates have served as reasonably effective shock absorbers. As the IMF cautiously put it: "On the whole, exchange rate flexibility appears to have enabled the world economy to surmount a succession of disturbing events, and to accommodate divergent trends in costs and prices in national economies with less disruption of trade and payments than a system of par values would have been able to do" [25]. FERs' greatest achievement is a negative one: floating made it possible for the world monetary system to avoid the general collapse that would have portended had fixed rates still been bolted in place when the gales came.

On the other side of the ledger, there is a long list of debits—many admittedly with question marks after them. The money markets continue to be susceptible to capital flows that move frequently, and in large enough volume, to force appreciable rate fluctuations; speculation clearly has not been self-equilibriating and stabilizing. Erratic and oscillating rate shifts have become a fixture of international monetary life. However, as yet, they have not significantly impeded commerce—largely, it appears, because trade is far less elastic that had been presumed. (The morale for the theorist *cum* policy adviser is obvious. If you are going to be wrong, be sure to make two errors that are offsetting—i.e., the effects of unexpectedly volatile rates are neutralized by surprisingly insensitive price mechanisms and inelastic trade.) It is still an open question whether rate instability—and apparent distortion of certain rates—will result in damaging structural maladjustments and resource misallocations. As for inflation, the case against floating is gaining in persuasiveness. Given the upward price bias of the modern economy, arbitrary rate changes cannot fail to push the inflation index. Insecure money also encourages price rises and wage claims. Furthermore, the failure of FERs to produce the promised payments equilibrium has resulted in that widespread resort to private capital markets which is cited as a major cause of the sudden growth in world liquidity—itself an inflationary development.

Finally, the expected independence of domestic policy from external constraints has proved illusory. The thorough integration of capital markets means that money breaches the walls of monetary insulation; continuing payments difficulties make governments sensitive to comparative, short term interest rates; and under a system of managed floating each nation must concern itself with what sort of management the other fellow is doing. The right to independent economic policies is still bought at a price—which can be actual vulnerability.

What are the prospects that the floating rate system will stabilize itself, and on what terms? What sort of government policies are needed to achieve it? What would the implications be for cross-national cooperation among monetary officials?

Key currency stability is probably the essential nucleus for a stable system. Fluctuations in the dollar-deutschemark-sterling rates are the primary reason for erratic exchange movements. Harold Cleveland has presented the persuasive argument that speculation is tied to expectations of long swings in currency values—especially, today, in the dollar-mark rate. His analysis estimates that the mark has been 30 percent above an equilibrium point "that would match the dollar's domestic buying power with that of the DM" [26]. Since other Eurosnake currencies, and the Swiss franc, are aligned directly or indirectly with the mark, they too are overvalued. Central banks, including those in Britain and Italy, "support their currencies at intervention points based on a weighted average" distorted by the unnaturally depressed dollar, so that the pound and lira as well, have been excessively high vis-à-vis the dollar [27].

The exchange markets have shown signs of an anxiety neurosis about the dollar, rooted in the earlier trauma of devaluation and inconvertibility, and in the vivid speculative runs that have left an enduring imprint on the minds of holders of external liquid assets. Ironically, the dollar plays a more important international role as a medium of exchange than it did in 1971, even as confidence in it remains depressed. This discrepancy explains much about its present weakness on the exchanges. The dollar overhang, estimated at $110 billion in 1970, is now somewhere between $250 and 300 billion—reflecting large, dollar-denominated oil payments and the pyramiding effect of the burgeoning Eurocurrency market. In a market saturated with dollars, the move by OPEC countries to diversify their currency portfolios "by selling dollars for strong European currencies" [28] coupled with the decision to calculate oil prices in SDRs, naturally depressed the dollar rate. Taken together, these actions could only confirm widespread doubts about the dollar's future. Yet, the dollar remains the medium of payment for oil, and for most other commodities of international exchange as well.

It is a classic chicken-and-egg problem. Consolidation of the unsettling overhang depends on restoration of confidence in the dollar. As soon as the dollar begins to look solid, and its exchange rate begins to move up, it becomes a more attractive currency all across the board—for investment, for currency portfolios, as the denomination in which the great multinationals hold their operating capital—and also the preferred denomination of oil producers. With the restoration of purchasing power parity, price changes themselves would gradually absorb excess dollars. In this view, such a turnaround in the speculative tide also would override the movement of interest-sensitive capital since "interest rate differentials cause funds to move internationally [and exchange rates to move] only if they coincide with speculative expectations" [29].

For this scenario to take shape, a fundamental symmetry has to be achieved between performance of the American and German economies, and policies must be synchronized [30]. Similar inflation rates, proportionate levels of money creation and strong payments positions would create conditions conducive to keeping the dollar-DM parity in line. As the core currencies for their respective monetary zones, they already serve as the reference points for monetary policy within each bloc. Stability between the two currencies thus militates strongly toward interzonal stability. While such a regularizing of their relationship might not be sufficient in itself to assure a calming of the exchanges, it would be a very important step in that direction. Follow the leader policies presume inequality; but abandoning the fiction of monetary equality and national freedom under floating is probably a condition of overall stability.

As a practical matter, German-American cooperation—as the centerpiece of a strategy for maintaining orderly rate movements—has two requirements. First is a recognition by both governments that it is vitally important for them to assume the responsibility of international economic leadership. The primary obligation, of course, is that of the United States so long as the dollar continues to perform special functions in the world monetary system. Complacency encouraged by the size and relative imperviousness of the American economy has too readily in recent years translated into a bland optimism that all will work out for the best. More active concern for the deleterious consequences of neglect is in order. The American attitude undoubtedly has helped nurture more self-centered outlooks elsewhere. In Germany, gradual release from the obsession with past guilt has modified her principled internationalism of the postwar years. She has become more "hard-headed" about pursuing her own interests. For both countries, the internal strains of stagflation have tended to reduce their governments' freedom of action. Hence, the very conditions that underscore the importance of extensive cross-national cooperation inhibit the promulgation of policies pointed in that direction.

Harmonization of monetary policy also implies close coordination intragovernmentally. Exchange rate management becomes a shared responsibility of central banks intervening on the markets and economics ministers designing programs of economic steering domestically. Monetary policy is of course one of two prime instruments of internal management. The reuniting of monetary policy's domestic and payments objectives means that interest rates and money supply would be determined with almost as much attentiveness to capital flows and exchange rates as to aggregate demand management. (In the United States, 1975 witnessed for the first time an admission by a Federal Reserve Chairman that the Bank's attitude toward money creation was taking into account external considerations.) Floating, which was supposed to insulate governments from payments constraints, can only work when domestic policies are closely coordinated.

By according a higher priority to exchange stability as an end in itself, such an approach should lessen the strains visible in some governments—e.g., in the United States, between central bank officials striving to contain rate movements and a Treasury inclined to view rate stability as subordinate to other goals of American domestic and international economic policy. The importance each agency attaches to the plus-sum dimension of international monetary relations would tend to coincide. A too sanguine view, however, is not in order. Disagreements can be expected to continue. Monetary authorities' phobia about the evils of inflation makes them more favorably inclined toward austerity programs than most ministers with an elected constituency. They also are likely to call on acknowledged external obligations to push the outcome of intragovernmental debates in their preferred conservative direction. To the extent that governments fail to solve the present dilemma of stagflation, the short term compulsions of domestic policy, on the one hand, and the seeming requirements of exchange stability (prudent, noninflationary monetary policies), on the other, will be in a tug of war. Central banks, with their routine attentiveness to rate movements (and in the daily contact with counterpart authorities now officially authorized by the Rambouillet Economic Summit), would intervene as a matter of course in the reaffirmed interest of orderly markets. Economics Ministers, if they do not succeed in mastering domestic economic forces, will pursue policies whose external effects are inadvertent—whether they are contradicting, facilitating or just confusing the task of cooperative managed floating.

The unavoidable paradox of today's interdependent conditions is that the operative principles of commerce and finance assume a functionally integrated world economy, although in fact national governments are unprepared to let it register the results in the distribution of wealth and resources. Nor are they ready to establish the institutions that could manage economic forces on the global plane at which they exist. The consequent strains and contradictions assure that no exchange rate system will perform optimally (perhaps not even well) and instead will pose a constant challenge to governments striving to maintain a semblance of regularity and stability.

NOTES TO CHAPTER 5

1. C.J. Morse, speech to the International Monetary Conference, "The Evolving Monetary System," Williamsburg, Virginia, June 7, 1974.

2. Charles Kindleberger, "Lessons of Floating Exchange Rates" (Paper presented to the Carnegie-Mellon/Rochester University Monetary Conference, November 15, 1974), p. 2.

3. Jacques R. Artus, "The Behavior of Manufactured Export Prices" (Paper

presented at Conference on Effects of Exchange Rate Adjustments, U.S. Treasury Department, Washington, D.C., April 4–5, 1974).

4. International Monetary Fund, *International Monetary Reform.* Documents of the Committee of Twenty (Washington, D.C., 1974).

5. Morse, "The Evolving Monetary System."

6. Federal Reserve Bank, *Monthly Review*, March 1975. See also its *Semi-Annual Report*, July 1975.

7. Alfred Hayes, "Emerging Arrangement in International Payments—Public and Private" (Per Jacobsson Lecture, August 1975), IMF, Washington, D.C., pp. 16–17.

8. *New York Times*, March 24, 1975.

9. *New York Times*, May 23, 1975.

10. Alan Teck "Foreign Exchange," *The Wall Street Transcript*, June 24, 1974.

11. *IMF Articles of Agreement*, Article IV, Section 4(a).

12. *IMF Guidelines for the Management of Floating Exchange Rates*, Decision No. 4232—(74/67), June 13, 1974.

13. Financial Survey, *Economist*, March 23–29, 1974.

14. Ibid.

15. IMF Annual Report, September 1975. Reported in the *New York Times*, August 24, 1975.

16. Estimates by Citibank reported in *Monthly Economic Letter*, June 1975. The problems of recycling generated a considerable literature, analytical and prescriptive. Two pieces in *Foreign Affairs* 53, 2 (January 1975) give the flavor of the discussion: Farmanfarmaian et al., "How Can The World Afford OPEC Oil?" and Hollis B. Chenery, "Restructuring The World Economy."

17. U.S. Treasury analysis in *Newsweek*, February 10, 1975.

18. Citibank, *Monthly Economic Letter*, June 1975. See also reports in the *New York Times*, July 22, August 31, 1975.

19. Remarks to the 1975 Annual Meeting of Governors reported in IMF *Survey* September 15, 1975, p. 151.

20. Simon, *Ibid.*, p. 150.

21. See the discussion by C. Fred Bergsten in "New Urgency For Monetary Reform," *Foreign Policy*, no. 19, Summer 1975.

22. Ibid., p. 83.

23. This idea has been propounded, and artfully developed, in the writings of professors Arthur B. Laffer and Robert A. Mundell. Their views are summarized and discussed by Jude Wanniski in an interpretive article, "The Mundell-Laffer Hypothesis—A New View of the World Economy," *Public Interest*, no. 39, Spring 1975.

24. Marina Whitman, "The Payments Adjustment Process and the Exchange Rate Regime: What Have We Learned" (Paper presented at the University of Pittsburgh, November 1974), p. 17.

25. IMF, *Annual Report*, 1975. The views of American international business are well expressed in "International Monetary Reform And Exchange Rate Management," Hearings Before the House Committee on Banking, Currency and

Housing and the Subcommittee on International Economics of the Joint Economic Committee, July 17, 18 and 21, 1975 (Washington, D.C.: U.S. Government Printing Office, 1975).

26. Citibank, *Monthly Economic Letter*, June 30, 1975.
27. Citibank, *Money International*, April 30, 1975.
28. Bergsten, "New Urgency," p. 23.
29. Citibank, *Money International*, April 30, 1975.
30. I am indebted to Harold Cleveland for emphasizing this point.

Conclusion

We introduced this study by outlining a number of theoretical issues about the way governments approach questtions of international economic policy. They grow out of a fundamental paradox. The problems facing governments today are comprehensive in scope and increasingly external in origin; yet the power to deal with them is dispersed among nations each with its own interests, circumstances and ways of handling its political affairs. Collective economic management runs the constant risk of being upset by intrusive national considerations and constructive initiatives of being stymied by domestic constraints—even assuming that there is the will to concerted action and the method known for meeting common system needs [1]. The central question we have been asking is whether the increasingly apparent dependence of internal ecoomic policy on world conditions, the unavoidable vulnerability to international forces, has so impressed itself on government leaders' perceptions of their country's interests that they are more inclined to overcome the parochialisms that impede achievement of collective purposes. The foregoing review and analysis of the events associated with the exchange crisis and creation of a flexible rate regime offers the opportunity to comment on this issue in relation to a major event with far-reaching implications.

We have been interested in what goes on inside governments as well as between governments. When faced with a serious disturbance in the external environment, we inquired as to what considerations and which officials favor the strengthening or extension of collaborative institutions. In adverse cirumstances, were the efforts of policymakers to reconcile domestic and international considerations appreciably affected by their involvement in networks for consultation and collaboration? More specifically, was there a noticeably greater internationalist orientation among central bankers who have explicit responsibilities for administering joint monetary arrangements? Did they have the inclination and opportunity to construct bureaucratic coalitions across national boundaries to press for commonly conceived solutions to disorderly exchange markets?

In Chapter 1 we hypothesized that certain features of their institutional role will lead monetary officials to be more attentive to the requirements for the efficient working of collective institutions—their direct participation in performing cooperative functions; the close professional ties thus fostered; their greater distance from partisan political pressures. We also formulated the reciprocal proposition that, in crisis situations, central policymaking organs move to impose their authority and decide matters left to specialized agencies in more tranquil times. The pattern of response to the 1973 exchange crisis largely confirms both these hypotheses. Central bankers do have pronounced feelings about the primacy of international monetary stability. It is also true that their political superiors are quick to intervene in order to assure that the former act in conformance with the nation's interests as elected officials define it.

Politicization, though, is not a simple process wherein a crude national interest is installed as the sole basis for judgment. Leaders are concerned about many things in addition to immediate domestic economic welfare—their security, their international status and the external relations that sustain all three. Hence, their involvement can force linkages between specific economic issues and overarching political concerns. Whether the linkage is a catalyst or a hindrance to problem solving depends on whether strong feelings about the broader political interest point in the same direction as the logic of economic cooperation. At both planes of policy, controversy is as likely to arise over the most effective ways to reach an agreed goal as over power and interest conflicts. The task that frustrated political leadership confronting the exchange crisis was that of defining the common interest and finding the method to satisfy it, as well as to compromise competing economic stakes in the outcome.

What does the governments' handling of the exchange crisis, and their strategies of reform, say about the will and capacity of nations to conduct their collective business? The most general conclusion to be drawn from this review is that the inherent strains and contradictions of the present situation work against structural innovation and strongly militate toward partial solutions and meliorative measures.

Reform strategies on the systemic scale at which monetary problems exist depend above all on national leaders with a talent for inspiring grand schemes and the skill to carry them through to realization. Monetary authorities, for their part, might be more or less nationalistic, their intentions more or less enlightened, their latitude for taking independent initiatives more or less tightly drawn according to national practice. But their freedom to prepare, and their power to implement proposals with the potential for settling framework issues or altering the powers of their governments, is narrowly circumscribed by the highest elected officials.

During the crisis period in March 1973, and then again in July, national leadership did come to the fore. Issues were politicized. Their intervention was probably absolutely necessary to reach the accord on floating. Despite the powerful situational logic in its favor, if the matter had been left to monetary officials, the strong distaste most central banks felt for floating rates in all likelihood would have blocked the reform (or, as seems more probable, resulted in disorderly competitive rate management). But political involvement was neither sustained long enough, nor agreed in the fundamental premises of how the world monetary order should be structured, for a new format to be put in place. Once the immediate danger had been overcome, political attention drifted elsewhere. (France, because of her dissatisfaction with the results, was an exception.) Indeed, there was not even a clear understanding as to how the float would work: could it, should it, be managed? Would monetary authorities aim at rough equilibrium points? Defined by what criteria? Under what, if any, instruction? None of these questions was answered in the course of political leadership's crisis management. As of this writing, two and one-half years later, there is still no accord as to whether flexible exchange rates are to be a permanent or interim arrangement, the guidelines for central bank intervention and the importance of harmonizing domestic policies in support of exchange operations.

Because an issue is politicized does not mean that it will stay politicized through to its resolution. Political will is not constant, but intermittent—of varying intensity and duration. The exchange crisis became the object of government concern because it promised very unpleasant effects. It remained at the top of the policy agenda only until that danger was dispelled (or pushed back beyond the horizon). Political will is always a quixotic element. Leaders are conserving of their authority. The normal disinclination to commit themselves to wideranging ventures is reinforced when the problems are technically daunting and the proposed plans unpersuasive. Then the status quo acquires an appeal incommensurate with its performance. The less accommodating reality is to simple solutions, the greater the disposition to restrict attention to remedial measures applied to immediate and specific needs. Conversely, the hesitancy of national leaders to take up the challenge of seeking new ways to master the forces of international economic life is encouraged by doubts as to the workability and effectiveness of the alternatives being discussed. For failure threatens disruption of the fragile and carefully equilibriated system of group reward and social welfare that rests in their political care.

CENTRAL BANK COLLABORATION

We had postulated that one possible spur to institution building might come from monetary authorities in the central banks. Their relative autonomy, as well as their concrete responsibilities for the system's monetary infrastructure, could be seen as permissive of bolder planning and encouraging of comprehensive attempts at resolving some of the system's contradictions. Further, their active collaboration on a transgovernmental basis suggested that they conceivably might opt for the internationalist route out of their common dilemma. Such an approach could entail (1) extending the powers of extant organizations like the IMF to establish more explicit rules to govern adjustment procedures, to provide surveillance of international currency markets and to regulate the growth of international liquidity; and/or (2) a thoroughgoing harmonization of national policies. Two questions were asked about what was in fact the dominant attitude and behavior of central bankers: One, how closely did they approximate an image of them as internationally minded institution builders? The other, what leeway did they have to indulge these impulses, if they indeed existed?

The Central Bank Ethos

Central bank directors are, in some respects, unique among economic officials. As Robert Russell has described elsewhere, they constitute a rather special fraternity of official fellows who do share a common fund of ideas about how the monetary world operates and what is needed for its orderly working [2]. This fraternity has multiple sources. Parallelism of function, similar if not identical responsibilities, analagous political and organizational circumstances and ambitions create a rapport that only those permitted of the same experiences can fully share. It produces a guild solidarity wherein one receives support, encouragement or consolation as the vicissitudes of monetary affairs might indicate. Their complementary approaches to problems of monetary management are rooted in a common understanding of the world in which they live and work, part of whose care is their responsibility. It is striking how closely attuned central bank directors are in their political philosophies and in the coordinates of their cognitive maps of the monetary universe, as well as in their preferences for certain procedures (informal consultation) and certain operational codes (stressing confidentiality and trust) for conducting their official business.

Although each gives an individual accent to these ideas that reflects professional analysis as much as national identity and institutional form, more evident is the extent to which their beliefs coincide. The models of economic reality (as framed in their explanations of how inflation, imprudent monetary policies and loss of confidence in money produced the 1973 exchange crisis) and their ideology (sound money is the cornerstone of economic progress and social justice) are fashioned into remarkably similar intellectual positions. While the agreement is not so total as to exclude differences of opinion on specific policy questions, the acceptance of a common paradigm for analysis and evaluation and the use of a common currency of intellectual exchange do facilitate productive deliberations, favor the development of a common position and create a strain toward consensus.

In large measure, this communality is fashioned from the experience of cooperation in working the Bretton Woods system and their positive judgment of its proficiency. Past achievements inspire confidence in the correctness of present arrangements and an optimistic estimate of their ability to manage successfully the system of capital transfers, exchange mechanisms and credit provision they superintend. In a sense, then, the fraternity of central bankers is contextually defined—i.e., its solidarity derives from the viability of that system. When confronted with a failing in its performance, the natural reaction of monetary authorities is to rededicate themselves to its principles, while suggesting how established procedures can be made to deal with the problem. At the same time, they are prone to reject alternatives that contradict those principles.

Of course, a common view of the world normally is easier to sustain when the policies drawn from it are working reasonably well. Or, to put it somewhat differently, disagreements can be minimized when all the participants are deriving benefits from administering present policies. These benefits take the form of enhanced professional pride, the economic achievements of their countries and the acknowledged authority of the agencies they direct. The test of solidarity, in outlook and action, comes when established ideas and institutions are called into question. In the response to strong pressures for change and innovation, one also gets a surer feel as to whether there exists a predisposition in favor of a collective international response to outstanding problems that has a meaning above and beyond the merely expedient recognition of the pragmatic need for routine coordination.

In the exchange crisis, a measure of disagreement and conflict did emerge. The dispute over how tightly the float should be managed brought to the surface rather basic differences as to the virtues of applying a pure free market philosophy to the currency exchanges. The differences of opinion between Dr. Emminger (with some sympathy from his Dutch colleague de Lannup) and most other central bankers reflected divergent perspectives compounded of doctrinal belief, technical analysis and conception of national interest. While not readily apparent so long as the par value system functioned smoothly, its collapse made these difference serious points of contention.

The exchange episode at the same time provides little evidence of an inclination to use the occasion of a system failure to advance significantly the range and depth of transgovernmental cooperation, building on the substantial foundation of present practical endeavors. Whatever concerting of action did take place, it was directed at maintaining stable conditions within the existing framework. The emphasis is on utilizing the established procedures of operational coordination—e.g., through renewed intervention on the exchanges (as has been done since July 1973) or consultation (by urging on their governments the importance of setting corresponding interest rates). On occasion, central bank directors did go so far as to take part in simultaneous advisory efforts that ran counter to the thinking of their heads of government—as was the case when the Bundesbank and the Bank of England joined together to resist the Brandt-Heath idea for British participation in the "snake." Given the easy relations that exist among central bankers, it is not surprising that their advising would not stay in watertight compartments but rather result in a communication of information and intentions. Whether one is prepared to label this behavior transgovernmental lobbying or coalition building is of more academic than practical importance. The exercise of influence was real (if not necessarily critical), it was keyed to a common view of the collective monetary interest and it had an undeniable, if not critical, bearing on the decision. It is noteworthy that this outstanding example of collaboration was aimed at thwarting a policy initiative that would have deepened institutional cooperation. A European Monetary Union carried the real possibility that formal cross-national institutions would be set up, partially superseding the old, informal network of consultation. There is no equivalent example of a central bank initiative that had broad potential for developing new structures of cooperation. In other instances, cooperation took the form of parallel efforts to preserve the integrity of prevailing arrangements and procedures for intergovernmental coordination.

The unreceptiveness to new internationalist undertakings has a number of causes: (1) conscientious doubts as to the technical feasibility and political acceptability of an innovation that involves extranational institutions (whether the grand idea of a world monetary authority to regulate a world currency or the somewhat more modest one of centrally administered capital controls), an attitude that reflects (2) deeply conservative social philosophies stressing stability and continuity that accord greater importance to domestic restraint than to expansionist policies that are seen as the source of international instability and, eventually, as demanding the implementation of untried (and therefore suspect) experiments in international planning; (3) a procedural conservatism that relies heavily on the personal judgment and authority of monetary officials; and (4) an "internationalism" that, while placing premiums on interstate cooperation, sees the self-defined and accountable authority of national governments as the precondition for accomplishing basic economic and political purposes—and which believes that collective action must be founded on the solidity and viability of the nation-state.*

We should remind ourselves that this question of whether, and to what degree, national officials with international functions act in support of measures to transcend national authority has a somewhat different practical meaning for those officials who are rooted in the national system than it does for members of a pre-existing supranational body such as the European Community. For the latter, organizational missions and programmatic achievement are measured, at least partly, by their progress in strengthening supranational authority. This is not at all the case for central bankers. Bureaucracy normally is a conserving force, unless the purpose defined for it by

*Organizational structures on an international scale are particularly unattractive since they evoke pressures for a formal symmetry of power among the members that is contrary to effective, coordinated management. Richard Cooper has succinctly made this point: "To the extent that asymmetries of treatment are important for efficient functioning, informal arrangements are therefore likely to be superior to formal arrangements that emerge from a negotiating process. In the international monetary sphere, an English-style constitution, built up through a series of acceptable practices, may be both easier to attain and even superior in content to a fully negotiated American-style constitution" [3].

political authority is directed explicitly toward a change in the status quo—e.g., the Rome accords. There is nothing in the mandate of central banks, in their individual or collective capacities, that represents an intergovernmental commitment to monetary integration.

The twin features then of the central bank approach to the exchange crisis were (1) to leave intact the present, nationally focused structure of cooperation; and (2) to reiterate their salient role in managing global monetary problems and preserving their powers for doing so. Monetary authorities hold to a deep faith in the essential importance of their supervisory and interventionist role, which introduces a modicum of order and predictability into what they see as basically a highly unstable economic universe.

Few economic officials in most Western countries—and certainly not central bankers—are confirmed planners with a penchant for subjugating contingencies to preconceived models and plans. They are intellectually skeptical of any such effort and by political conviction disinclined to accept either the practicality or desirability of attempting it. Seasoned judgment is the commodity in which they place greatest stock. However, the intelligent use of that judgment depends on creating conditions of continuity and in preserving the institutional tools that prudent thinking guides. The crisis of 1973 was threatening to render impossible, and indeed superfluous, just the sort of restrained monetary management that was their forte and raison d'être. (Accordingly, it was only to be expected that central bank officials—in sharp contrast to the academic champions of floating—did not view the switchover to flexible exchange rates as that epochal change in the world's monetary structure that would usher in a new day of market-based stability and progress. Surely, they foresaw no prospect of their own relegation to the scrapheap of international monetary history—an idea so appealing to free market apostles.)

Central Banks and Treasuries

The very real differences that in some instances were observable between central bankers and their Treasury colleagues (the United States being the one outstanding example) were only exceptionally attributable to fundamentally different expectations of what floating could or could not accomplish. Nor was bureaucratic rivalry the overriding source of conflict. Differences cannot be reduced to the imperative of organizational self-preservation on the part of central banks and the desire of Treasuries to trim the sails of privateering directors while imposing political discipline on their freewheeling international networks. Both of these elements were there, in the

American case. The crux of the dispute, however, was the substantive policy question of deciding what national advantages could, or should, be sought from an unstable situation. It was a situation where doing nothing promised a favorable turn of events (a dollar depreciation); while doing something (reintervening) was, at best, of dubious effectiveness for restoring stability. Priorities differed; political responsibilities and sensitivities varied; and, therefore, so did tactical judgments of when and how obligations should be met. The inconclusiveness of technical analyses assured that even appeal to some presumed objective truth was out of the question.

At those times of pronounced disagreement, there was never any doubt as to where paramount authority lay. It was the cabinet officer, supported by elected leadership, who prevailed. Where changes were forced in centrally decreed policy (as with the American concession to resume support of the dollar in July 1973), they were induced mainly by pressures from friendly governments and by a dawning awareness of the manifestly disruptive effects of a stubborn refusal to change its mind. The arguments of internal opponents, even so prestigeous a one as the chairman of the Federal Reserve Board, were of secondary importance. Whatever the influence of officials in intramural jousts on policy matters of this nature—influence, we should be reminded, that varied markedly from country to country, although not negligible in any—there clearly did not exist that margin for central bank maneuver and initiative as to permit transgovernmental coalition building in support of major innovation—even if, contrary to their inclination, they had favored a dramatic initiative. There is no evidence to be adduced from this study that contradicts the conclusion of Robert Russell, based on a series of earlier episodes, that "transgovernmental coalitions among central bankers and working-level officials were increasingly constrained even before the events of 1971, as monetary issues became more controversial" [4].

The differences in approach between monetary authorities and other national officials can be overdrawn. Indeed, in some governments (the British and French) there often was a near identity of view. More important, for the most part they share a nationally focused outlook on international economic questions which is at once scornful of supranational answers and suspicious of a truly free market strategy. The latter would offer no assurance of consistent outcomes and is seen as carrying enormous potential for disruption. The loss by national governments of the power to control—however imperfectly—their external monetary environment was anathema, both for fear of changes that could contradict national ends and out of principled opposition to any proposal that would remove from their hands the power of economic decision. The market approach, like the supranational approach, violated that principle; and, unlike the latter, it lacked even the promised benefits of central management. Economic managers as a whole have a proclivity for order and regularity. They prefer to operate in a world of recognizable, if not always predictable, quantities. The desire to proceed with confidence in a reasonably constant environment explains the widespread skepticism about floating rates.

THEORISTS AND PRACTITIONERS

What role did economic theory play in the decision to introduce flexible exchange rates? The formal analysis of the academic theorist can perform four functions—to illuminate a problem and the conditions associated with it; to offer the analytic formula for solving the problem and achieving a policy objective; to confirm an approach taken expediently or pragmatically by policymakers and favored for reasons that have more to do with its convenience, philosophic congeniality or the preferential benefits it promises (in this way, the academic model provides "technical legitimation"); to be used in disparaging other prospective approaches and proposals which are viewed as undesirable for any of the aforementioned reasons.

Elucidation of the par value system's vulnerabilities and weaknesses had been the collective pastime of academics and reflective officials for a decade before its eventual demise. The light shed on these suspect properties of the system was focused by practitioners and theorists in constant dialogue with each other. The broad conditions that underlay the crisis were all topics that had been examined with a fine-toothed comb. Whatever the real differences in weighting the various factors in the equation, and disagreements over particulars, it cannot be said that policymakers were traveling unmapped terrain or ignorant of the long-standing and well-publicized advice of assorted trailmasters. There was little in the way of new insights, new angles of vision, new ways of conceptualizing matters that were not part of the common intellectual stock in 1973.

As for the proximate cause of the crisis—speculative capital movements—it required no formidable analytical power or brilliant imagination to notice and understand. Earlier awareness of the potential that was being created for disruptive money flows by liquidity accumulation on the Eurocurrency market would have been useful. In fact, there were few at the university or in the council chamber who were not negligent in their slowness to perceive what was happening. But the lack was of foresight, not theory. More complete and accurate information about the volume of mobile capital at loose, how it was distributed and how those in control of it were conducting their affairs perhaps could have been beneficial—assuming an ability to use it effectively. In this respect, central bank officials did not distinguish themselves by the avidity with which they sought to uncover the data (and might also be accused of a certain hubris in assuming they had the situation well in hand).

As for the theory of flexible exchange rates itself, it was never truly accepted as formulated. We have recounted how most government officials remained dubious about many of the technical assessments and judgments that were the underpinning for the case in support of floating and skeptical of claims for its curative powers. The period of active proselytization did, however, have the effect of preparing the ground by intellectually acclimatizing the international monetary community to the idea. It also pinpointed possible trouble spots. When the juncture was reached where all other alternatives for dealing with the situation had been exhausted or rejected as impractical, there were "flexible exchange rates" all packaged and waiting. The pure theory was less impressive than expedient considerations were pressing.

Thus the elaborate intellectual superstructure girding the case for free floating was largely immaterial to the decision. The diffuse process through which it was constructed and debated over the years can be seen as providing technical legitimation. Even in this regard, the need for such scientific laying on of hands was less acute than is often felt by policymakers. In this arcane field, the popular constituency would defer to any reasonable proposals propogated with assurance. The knowing constituency—speculators, traders, private bankers and government officials—were attuned to the practical implications of floating and aware of what the decision foreshadowed in the way of continuing central bank involvement in rate management.

Theorists and practitioners do not meet as intellectual strangers. There is a community of discourse and familiarity of position that assures mutual comprehension. If there are occasional problems of communication, they are to be found in differences of professional perspective and role. It is the bias of the academic to express complex problems as logical puzzles. There is an undeniable strain between the requirements of parsimonious, unitary theory and the inherent contradictions and paradoxes of the real world. The unfortunate tendency to reify models is too often the answer to the problem of making theory proximate to policy decisions. As Professor Haberler has posed the issue: "If, on the one hand, we base our analysis on more or less reasonable assumptions, we have to be content with rather uncertain and at best approximate results. If, on the other hand, we are looking for unambiguous results, we are forced to make specific, and, usually, not generally applicable assumptions, or, at any rate, assumptions that are difficult to prove" [5]. Recognition of this problem is the first requirement of relevant expert advising.

The official, by contrast, is interested above all in solving a policy problem, not theoretical ones. He has his own intellectual biases and ideology, but they are under constant assault by the pragmatic constraints of his office and the challenge of real life conditions. Public officials, therefore, are not necessarily desirous for, or in need of, the most systematic and sophisticated economic analysis or the most intricate and subtly nuanced strategy for reform. Often, they are on the prowl for quick fixes. Normally, they are reluctant to pronounce themselves avowed adherents to one particular theory or school of thought. They are keen to avoid being locked into a mode of analysis or approach whose doctrinal rigidities would limit their freedom to make selective and discriminating use of a theory's postulates as it might suit their policy needs. This practical interest in keeping open one's analytical options is reinforced for monetary officials by the carefully cultivated image of the central banker who relies on his experienced judgment more than formal analysis in performing his functions as monetary manager.

MORALE AND PROSPECT

The exchange crisis has been revealing of the dilemma that confronts, and often puzzles, those accountable for the performance of the world's monetary system. There is the constant tug of domestic conditions that blurs vision of mutual interdependencies and which hampers attempts to get at collective problems. The almost daily struggle to meet the concerns of ever anxious political constituencies leaves little time to contemplate international conditions in their full complexity. There are the real conflicts of national interests and purposes, the equally troublesome imagined ones and the uncertainty as to which are which. There is also the obvious inadequacy of extant international organizations for regulating the system's monetary affairs and the deep reluctance to accord them powers commensurate to the collective task.

Overlaying all of these elements, and inhibiting all action, are pervasive doubts as to the proper shape of any new arrangements and the efficacy of proposals for improving system performance. Effects are unclear and unpredictable. There is little assurance that you "can get there from here"—even assuming that you know exactly where you are. Any significant reform venture in the monetary field trails question marks as to whether it will work in system terms and whether it will produce comparable improvements in the welfare of its several national components.

It is not in the style of national leadership in modern democracies to stake domestic welfare on chancy bets. They have small appetite for major innovation or schemes of international institution building. Officials, elected or permanent, political or bureaucratic, follow a "sufficing" mode of policymaking. That is to say, there are ingrained habits and preferences that eschew the quest for optimal solutions in favor of ones that are politically viable and of proven administrative practicality and that do not demand a drastic alteration of prevailing beliefs nor put in doubt established procedures and prerogatives of government. As clearly demonstrated on the exchange crisis, and as borne out by the recent history of monetary reform generally, there is a strong propensity to limit and to contain wherever possible. In considering a proposed reform, an official implicitly asks three questions: Will it permit the present system to keep "ticking over" and the benefits flowing? Does it promise to increase benefits, on an absolute or comparative national scale? What are the costs in relinquishing, perhaps permanently, some slice of autonomous power (or increased uncertainty of performance) to achieve policy objectives? This is not the formula for dramatic change. Where the situation is confused and the path to national betterment obscure, political leaders will concentrate on those features they can discern and be all the more protective of those interests obviously at stake.

As yet, there has been nothing so apparent or compelling in the recurrent monetary crises as to render that approach untenable. Certainly the crises on the exchange markets, while seriously troubling, were not seen as precursors of a general system breakdown that would pose starkly the choice between grasping onto national powers of diminished potency (and accepting the consequences) or taking the plunge into the unchartered waters of monetary union, in some form or other. Without unmistakable evidence that such a collapse is in the offing, and lacking a persuasive alternative, officials invariably will try to make do with the existing system which, however flawed, has to its credit the still remarkable successes of the past generation.

NOTES TO CONCLUSION

1. The discrepancy between what is "rational" for the system as a functional whole and what is "rational" for its component national parts is acutely analyzed by Stephen D. Cohen, *International Monetary Reform, 1964–1969 The Political Dimension* (New York: Praeger, 1971).

2. Robert Russell, Transgovernmental Interaction In The International Monetary System, 1960–1972, *International Organization* XX (October 1973).

3. Richard N. Cooper, "Prelogomena To The Choice Of An International Monetary System," *International Organization,* vol. 29, no. 1, Winter, 1975.

4. Russell, p. 59.

5. Gottfried Haberler, "A Survey of International Trade Theory" (Special papers In International Economics, Princeton University, no. 1, July 1961).

Index

Bank of England 61, 63, 74–75, 105, 134
Bank for International Settlements (BIS) 9, 26, 54, 84–85
Banque de France 60, 82
Barber, Anthony 75
'Benign neglect' 24, 49
Bergsten, Fred 119
Brandt, Chancellor Willy 44, 73–74, 117, 134
Bretton Woods 11, 20–21, 61, 79, 133
Burke-Hartke Bill 55
Burns, Arthur 53–56, 76, 84

Carli, Guido 72–73
Cleveland, Harold van B. 123–124
Common Market 12–13
  monetary union 71–72, 73–76, 105, 134
Connolly, John 27, 49
Coombs, Charles 55, 84–85, 106
Cooper, Richard 135n.

Daane, Dewey 54
Deutsche Bundesbank 19, 42, 45–46, 74–75, 79, 100, 105

elasticities 94–96
Emminger, Otmar 42–43, 46, 78–79, 134
Eurodollar market 23, 47

Federal Reserve Bank 19, 51, 53–56, 105, 107, 109–110, 125, 137
Financial Times 78
Flanigan, Peter 83
Friedman, Milton 90

General Agreement to Borrow 43, 62
General Agreement on Trade and Tariffs (GATT) 4, 49, 52
de Gaulle, General Charles 57
Giscard d'Estaing, Valéry 57, 59–60, 78, 82, 113
Gilpin, Robert 57

Haberler, Gottfried 49n., 140
Hayes, Alfred 98, 109
Heath, Prime Minister Edward 74, 134
Houtakker, Hendrik 49

International Monetary Fund (IMF)
  postwar interdependence 4, 25, 47
  Group of Ten 26
  Committee of Twenty on Reform 29, 80
  March Crisis 77
  flexible exchange rates 88, 94, 104, 112–114, 121–122
  oil-facility 116–117
Inflation
  exchange crisis 42–44
  flexible exchange rates 119–122
  stagflation 97–99
Interest Equalization Tax 23
Irwin, Ambassador 83

June-July Crisis 81–85
Jobert, Foreign Minister Michel 82n.
Johnson Harry 96

Keohane, Robert O. 7
Kissinger, Henry A. 50, 82n., 116–117
Klassen, Karl 46, 79

Machlup, Fritz 20n., 90–91
McKinnon, Ronald 92n.
Le Monde 30, 81
Morse, Jeremy 29, 103, 104

Nixon, President Richard N. 48–51
Nye, Joseph S. 7

Oil price-rise 114–119
Organization for Economic Corporation and Development (OECD)
 postwar interdependence 4
 Economic Policy Committee 26, 114
Organization of Petroleum Exporting Countries 114–119
Ortoli, François-Xavier 73

Peterson, Peter 51–52, 55
politicization 13–16
Pompidou, President Georges 57, 60

Rambouillet 'Economic Summit' 106, 113, 126
Reuss, Henry 110n.
Rolfe, Sidney and Burtle, James L. 49n.
Russell, Robert W. 132, 137

Sato, Prime Minister 65
Schmidt, Hans. O. 22n.
Schmidt, Helmut 44, 46
Schultz, George 49, 52–55, 73, 76–78, 82, 84
Simon, William 97n., 109, 116
Smithsonian Agreement 27, 28, 105, 108
Special Drawing Rights (SDRs) 4, 21, 27, 119, 124
La Stampa 72
Stein, Herbert 83
Steinbruner, John 31
'Swaps' 20, 71

The Times of London 30, 81, 83
Transgovernmental Politics 7–8
Triffin, Robert 21
Tüngler, Johannes 83, 85, 106

Vernon, Raymond 22
Volcker, Paul 51, 55, 72

Whitman, Marina vN. 97, 121
Wilson, Prime Minister Harold 62
Witteveen, Johannes 97, 113, 116, 118
Wormser, Olivier 60, 82

About the Author

Michael Brenner has written in a number of public policy fields. This study was prepared while he was a Fellow at the Center For International Affairs, Harvard University. Prof. Brenner is the author of *Technocratic Politics & The Functionalist Theory of European Integration*, and *The Political-Economy of America's Environmental Dilemma*. His articles on international politics have appeared in *International Organization*, *World Politics*, *Comparative Politics*, *International Affairs*, *The International Studies Quarterly*, and other journals. He has taught at Cornell, Stanford, the University of California (Berkeley) and Boston University.